Radical
Christian Communities

D1390132

Radical
Christian Communities

by

Thomas P. Rausch, S.J.

A Michael Glazier Book
THE LITURGICAL PRESS
Collegeville, Minnesota

About the Author

Rev. Thomas P. Rausch, S.J. is Professor of Theology and Rector of the Jesuit Community at Loyola Marymount University in Los Angeles. He is a member of both the Theological Commission and the Ecumenical Commission of the Archdiocese of Los Angeles. He is also a member of the Los Angeles Lutheran Roman Catholic Committee and the Los Angeles Catholic Evangelical Dialogue. Father Rausch's teaching areas include New Testament, ecclesiology, christology, and ecumenism. He is the author of *The Roots of the Catholic Tradition* (Michael Glazier, 1986) and *Authority and Leadership in The Church* (Michael Glazier, 1989).

A Michael Glazier Book

published by

THE LITURGICAL PRESS

Typography by Brenda Belizzone and Mary Brown.
Cover design by David Manahan, O.S.B.

1   2   3   4   5   6   7   8   9

Library of Congress Cataloging-in-Publication Data

Rausch, Thomas P.
    Radical Christian communities / by Thomas P. Rausch.
        p.   cm.
    "A Michael Glazier book."
    Includes bibliographical references and index.
    ISBN 0-8146-5008-2
    1. Christian communities—History. 2. Monasticism and religious
order—History. I. Title.
    BV4405.R38   1990
    271—dc20   90-43767
                                                        CIP

Contents

❧

For the six Jesuits
of the Jesuit Community
Universidad Centroamericano
Jose Simeon Canas,

Segundo Montes,
Ignacio Ellacuría
Ignacio Martín-Baró
Joaquin López y López
Juan Ramon Moreno
Amando López

and their co-workers
Elba Julia Ramos
Celina Maricet Ramos

murdered in El Salvador
16 November 1989

In Memoriam

❧

ACKNOWLEDGEMENTS

Most books have personal beginnings. The seed for this one was planted by Jeff Dietrich, the leader of the Catholic Worker Community here in Los Angeles. We had been talking about the Catholic Worker and several other justice communities. After a number of conversations, I began to see the need for a book which could deal with contemporary Christian communities in the context of the rich history of Christian communities in the life of the church. Besides inspiring the project, Jeff provided pictures showing the life and iconography of the Catholic Worker.

Many others helped with the book in various ways, reviewing sections of the manuscript, helping me track down material, offering insights and providing pictures.

Two friends in Switzerland helped with the section on Grandchamp. Cathy Clifford shared with me her own studies on the history and spirituality of Grandchamp; she also provided some pictures. Sister Heidi supplied some material on the life of the community. For the warm welcome I have so often experienced there I am grateful to all the sisters of Grandchamp.

I am grateful to Brother John of Taizé for his helpful suggestions and pictures for the chapter on the Taizé community. I have been to Taizé a number of times, but his help was very important in attempting to capture the special spirit of this community.

When I visited Trosly Breuil in the summer of 1988 I approached the l'Arche community there with some anxiety, both because I don't speak French and because, like many others I suspect, I have never been very comfortable with mentally handicapped people. But there was no need for my anxiety. The welcome at l'Arche was simple, direct, and warm. Simone Landrien put me in touch with some important sources. David Rothrock, S.J., a Jesuit friend of many years past and now a member of the l'Arche Tehoma Hope community in Tacoma, Washington, shared a number of insights and gave me some pictures.

Brother Luke, the Local Servant for the Missionary Brothers of Charity in Los Angeles, described for me the life and vision of the brothers. Father Peter Hocken of the Mother of God Community, Gaithersburg, Maryland, put me in touch with sources and offered suggestions on what I had written on the covenant communities. A sister of the Monastery of Bethlehem, Livingston Manor, New York, was most generous in helping me present the Monastic Family of Bethlehem and the Assumption of the Virgin. Abbot Thomas Davis of the Abbey of New Clairvaux, Vina, California and the Reverend John Harvey, leader of the Iona Community in Scotland both provided pictures. Steve McKindley-Ward dug up for me some background on the Sojourners Community in Washington, D.C.

I am very grateful to all these men and women for allowing me to present something of their communities in this book. By their cooperation and contributions they have made the book possible. I have tried to be sensitive to their concerns. For the interpretation, the responsibility is my own.

Finally I would like to express my gratitude to a number of people at Loyola Marymount University. I am very grateful to the staff of the Charles Von der Ahe Library, especially to Jean Davis, for all the help in tracking down books and difficult to find articles. Michael Brodsky of the Department of Art and Art History shared his expertise in working with photographs. My colleagues in the Department of Theology sustained me with their interest. I am especially grateful to Michael Downey, who took time out of his Sabbatical to review the manuscript and to offer his always helpful and challenging comments.

To all those who contributed to this book in so many ways I offer my heartfelt thanks.

Thomas P. Rausch, S.J.

INTRODUCTION

One of the greatest horrors of the twentieth century is the holocaust, the systematic attempt of Nazi Germany to exterminate the Jewish people. By the end of the Second World War almost six million Jews had died in the extermination camps of the Third Reich. Another six million, comprised of Poles, Russians, Gypsies, homosexuals, the physically and mentally handicapped, and others who did not fit into Hitler's ideal Germany, had perished as well. How could this have happened?

Germany under the Nazis had no monopoly on mass murder. Genocide has happened more than once in the twentieth century. But what makes the crimes committed in Germany under the Nazis so difficult to comprehend is the fact that they took place in a nation so distinguished for both its faith and its culture.

Hitler did not seize power. He and his Nazi party were constitutionally elected. Some Christians protested Nazi policies and paid the price. According to William L. Shirer, who worked in Berlin as a reporter prior to World War II, thousands of Catholic priests, nuns, and lay leaders were arrested in the years before the war, mostly on trumped-up charges. In 1937, 808 Protestant pastors and lay leaders were arrested, most of whom were sent to concentration camps.[1]

But most Christians in Germany did not protest. As Johann Baptist Metz has written, German Christians went on praying and singing with their backs to Auschwitz.[2] Their Christianity and their churches failed; neither was a countercultural force sufficient to challenge the new national ideology of the Nazis.

Metz grew up in Germany during the Hitler years. He sees the failure of Christianity in Germany during the Second

World War as part of a much greater crisis. In modern times, he argues, "the messianic religion of the Bible has largely been changed into bourgeois religion."[3]

In Metz's view, modern Christianity has domesticated the radical Gospel of Jesus. Jesus' message was rooted in the prophetic tradition of Israel and in his own intense experience of God's call. In proclaiming God's messianic love Jesus, like the prophets, saw the poor as a privileged group. He stood in solidarity with all who were suffering and so submitted to suffering himself. And he called all who would listen to discipleship based on this messianic love. But in place of this radical discipleship what has emerged is a bourgeois religion, a cultural Christianity which by carefully distinguishing between public and private life, and thus, between politics and morality, legitimates a life of comfort and privilege at the expense of the radical meaning of the Gospel.

In every age of the church men and women have tried to respond to the Gospel's radical call to discipleship with Jesus and community with one another. In the early church there were women consecrated to virginity and martyrs who gave their lives for their faith; their enemies remarked on their love for one another. In the third and fourth centuries, when Christian life became not only legal, but also respected and even prosperous, many men and women left the cities to seek God anew in the silence of the desert. They often gathered together into communities which were the predecessors of the monastic families or orders.

Originally these were countercultural communities. They were intentional communities, part of a countercultural movement whose members sought to withdraw from the world, from what was common and conventional, in order to live out the Gospel with all its challenges. They gave up promising careers, stripped themselves of their possessions, chose to live celibate lives, and often promised obedience to a spiritual teacher. Thus they chose to live a life which stood at some critical distance from the surrounding culture. Because they wanted to root their lives unreservedly in the central metaphors which grounded the life of Jesus, their discipleship was a radical discipleship and their communities were radical communities. Such radical communities have appeared and flourished in every age of the church.

But their success has time and again been the cause of their undoing. With their stability and the industry of their members, these religious communities frequently became established and affluent themselves; the original vision of a radical discipleship was lost or compromised to conform to a lifestyle which had emerged or to support a work undertaken. They have often been in need of renewal, and just as often men and women of vision have sought to reform them, or to establish new communities, to live out more perfectly the call to discipleship in light of new circumstances and new times.

Our own age is no exception. In a time of increasing social isolation and fragmentation new communities have emerged, communities which have sought to embody the Gospel in a radical way, whether by being communities of peace and reconciliation, of social ministry and solidarity with the poor, of service to the church, or of prayer and contemplation. Some of them, like the base communities of Latin America, seek to be church in a new way by becoming churches of the poor. They differ in terms of their particular emphases. However all of them stand at some critical distance from the cultures within which their members live out their Christian lives, and so can be considered radical Christian communities.

In this book we will consider some of these radical Christian communities. But because these communities are not a novel phenomenon, but rather the current manifestation of an impulse deeply rooted in the Christian tradition and in the Gospel itself, we will approach them in this broader context.

We will begin with the radical Gospel of Jesus and his call to discipleship which the early Christians sought to live out, sometimes at the cost of their lives. Then we will consider the ascetic movement in the third and fourth century and the monasticism which developed from these hermits and cenobites who sought the face of God in the silence of the desert.

In the turmoil and upheavals which reshaped the life and geography of Europe in the twelfth and thirteenth centuries, new communities emerged which sought to combine evangelical poverty and witness with a common life in an increasingly urban culture. Many of these were lay movements. Others became new religious orders.

The sixteenth century Reformation attacked traditional

monastic and religious life. But it brought with it some radical attempts at Christian community within Protestantism as well as a renewal of religious life in the Catholic Counter Reformation.

Finally, in what will be our major focus, we will study a number of contemporary Christian communities, lay and religious. They do not represent the only way of living out the Gospel call to discipleship. The Christian life has many expressions. But these communities, like their predecessors, may have much to teach others who seek to live a life based on the Gospel today. In a world such as ours, where the symbols of Christianity have been so devalued, ignored, and forgotten, we need their witness.

1

The Radical Gospel

One of the difficulties about really hearing the words of Jesus in the gospels is that they are so familiar to us. We have read them or heard them proclaimed so many times that they have become routine, and so we frequently miss their real challenge. In this chapter we will consider some of those sayings of Jesus which suggest the radical nature of his message.

It is true that the gospels are not literal transcriptions of Jesus' words. They are the product of a long process of development and so often reflect the deeper understandings of the early Christian communities as they continued to preach and celebrate his message. Yet the words attributed to Jesus cannot simply be dismissed as the theology of one or other evangelist. As Schillebeeckx has pointed out in discussing the criteria for a critical recovery of the historical Jesus, sayings attributed to him by the primitive church may be grounded in his inspiration and orientation, for the gospels have the earthly Jesus as their norm and criterion.[1]

The Reign of God

Most people familiar with the Gospel tradition are aware that at its very center is Jesus' preaching of the coming of the kingdom or reign of God. For Jesus, God's reign was a dynamic event; it was not a place. He proclaimed in word and example that the reign of God was at hand. As a man of his times, Jesus drew upon his Jewish tradition for the images and concepts through which his message was expressed. But what precisely does this message of Jesus mean for us today? How can we translate it into a contemporary idiom while still remaining faithful to what Jesus himself taught?

Too often in history Christians have turned Jesus' preaching of the reign of God into another worldly religion with an individualistic doctrine of salvation. With the Gospel thus privatized, it is not difficult to see how a social critic like Karl Marx could describe Christianity as one more ideology of an unjust society which provided an "opium for the masses." But in recent years an increasing number of theologians have recovered for theology and the Christian life the radically social nature of the Gospel.

For Schillebeeckx, the message of Jesus was one of hope which contrasted strongly with the warning of an impending judgment preached by his predecessor, John the Baptist. John was a penitential preacher announcing God's wrath.[2] Jesus, on the other hand, brought good news (*euaggelion*); he proclaimed God's action now present within human history and in our own human lives. According to Schillebeeckx, God's presence and action is mediated by human beings, made visible in men and women caring for one another.[3]

In a remarkable little book entitled *Jesus before Christianity,* Albert Nolan argues that the kingdom of God that Jesus proclaimed was a kingdom of love and service which reveals God as a God of compassion. For Nolan it is precisely human compassion which "releases God's power in the world, the only power than can bring about the miracle of the kingdom."[4] Though Jesus did not found an organization, a movement grew up around him consisting of those who tried to live as he lived, organizing their own lives according to his values. This is what it truly means to acknowledge Jesus as Lord and savior.[5]

Jon Sobrino writes from the perspective of Latin American liberation theology. He describes Jesus as calling others to a radical discipleship which would place them at the disposal of the kingdom.[6] The commitment which this involves has obvious implications for the often oppressive societies in which so many Christians live. In the same vein, though in a European context, Johann Baptist Metz says that Jesus summons men and women to a messianic discipleship and love. To some, this messianic discipleship is a radical one; it "may look like treason—a betrayal of affluence, of the family, and of our customary way of life."[7]

Finally, from the perspective of a feminist hermeneutic, Elisabeth Schüssler Fiorenza describes the reign (*basileia*) of God as being realized wherever people are being healed, set free from oppression or dehumanizing power systems, and made whole.[8] She describes what she calls "the Jesus movement" as a "discipleship of equals," with implications for today's church.[9]

The emphasis on the social dimensions of the Gospel which is evident in these theologians and the profound critique of much of first world Christianity which accompanies it has alarmed many. They fear that the Gospel is being secularized, emptied of its transcendent dimension, turned into another revolutionary ideology. The criticism that some more conservative Protestant churches have directed against the World Council of Churches because of its support of Third World movements for political and economic liberation is one example of this. A similar concern can be seen among Roman Catholics, even at official levels. In a 1984 instruction on liberation theology issued by the Vatican's Sacred Congregation for the Doctrine of the Faith, the CDF cautioned against "the temptation to reduce to Gospel to an earthly gospel."[10]

Secularizing the Gospel is always a danger. But much greater is the danger of spiritualizing and privatizing it, ignoring the hard sayings about our responsibility to others, forgetting the stories which make us uncomfortable, turning precept into parable and challenge into consolation. Jesus himself was very much a man in the tradition of the Israelite prophets. Though he brought a message of hope to all people, his preaching was understood as being in a special way "glad tidings to the poor" (Lk 4:18).

To try and recapture something of the radical Gospel of Jesus we need to see his message in the context of the tradition out of which it comes. We will consider first the holiness and justice of the God of Israel; second, the emphasis on justice in the prophetic tradition; and finally, the social dimension of the Gospel of Jesus.

The Holy God of Israel

Unique to the Israelite experience of God is the profound sense that God is holy, and therefore the Israelites themselves, as members of God's people, are to be holy also. The Hebrew root *qds* from which the word holy comes suggests a cutting off or a separation from the ordinary or everyday, the profane. God is not like human beings; God is different, other, unique. When God draws near to Moses at the burning bush Moses must remove his shoes for the ground on which he stands is holy ground (Ex 3:5). So also the holy mountain of the Sinai theophany is shrouded in smoke and fire (Ex 19:18).

But God's holiness is more than physical; it is also moral. Therefore, the people with whom God has entered into covenant relationship must be holy. The Israelite "Holiness Code" (Lev 18-26), with its complex ritual and ethical laws, insists on this: "Be holy, for I, the Lord your God, am holy" (Lev 19:2).

The terms of the covenant, expressed most clearly in the Decalogue (Ex 20:1-17), spell out the parameters of living in covenant relationship with Yahweh. To worship false gods, dishonor parents, kill, steal, commit adultery, bear false witness, or covet what belonged to a neighbor was to step outside of the covenant relationship. Here the uniqueness of the Israelite experience of God comes into focus. Israel's neighbors understood themselves as having religious obligations to their gods which were fulfilled through ritual and cult. Their gods demanded obedience. But like the gods of Greek mythology, these gods were anthropomorphically conceived and so shared in the same faults as those who worshiped them. But Yahweh the God of Israel was holy and demanded that Israel be holy also.

Closely related to the concept of God's holiness is that of God's justice. The biblical emphasis on justice can sometimes be overlooked because some English translations have tended to use the word "righteousness" or "judgment" to translate the Hebrew *sedek*. Though *sedek* can convey either righteousness or the modern sense of justice, the social context in which the word frequently occurs indicates that justice is the more appropriate translation. For some scholars, a sense of Yahweh

as a God who demands a justice expressed through law pre-
dates its expression in the Decalogue (Ex 20:1-17). According
to John Topel it "appears probable ... that Israel from its
birth experience in Egypt understood that Yahweh was a
source of just precepts for Israel and that to be a true offspring
of Yahweh, Israel must practice justice."[11]

Israel's sense of God's justice cannot be understood apart
from its own experience of liberation from the economic and
political oppression in Egypt. Leaving Egypt with the Israelites
were other fugitive slaves and migrant workers, people from
other tribes, even some Egyptians (Ex 12:38). They were joined
later by other disadvantaged peoples, seminomads and small
farmers, in a movement which was to eventually wrest control
of Canaan from the minor kings who ruled its city-states.
What emerged from the exodus experience was a conviction
of God's special concern for the poor and the oppressed which
later found expression in Israel's legal traditions. The frequent
references to God's care for "the widow, the orphan, and the
stranger in the land" are evidence of this divine predilection:
"You shall not molest or oppress an alien, for you were once
aliens yourselves in the land of Egypt. You shall not wrong
any widow or orphan. If ever you wrong them and they cry
out to me, I will surely hear their cry" (Ex 22:20-22; cf. Lev
19:34; Deut 10:18-19; 16: 11-12). Therefore justice belongs
unmistakably to the requirements of the covenant.

This insistence on God's justice and on God's concern for
the poor and the oppressed runs throughout the biblical tradition. It is basic to the Torah or law as we have seen. It is
present in the Psalms (Pss 9:7-9; 10:17-18; 103:6; 146:7-9) and
in the Wisdom literature (Job 29:12-17; Prov 21:13; 29:7). But
it is especially with the prophets that God's concern for what
we call today social justice comes into focus.

Justice in the Prophetic Tradition

The classical prophets of the 8th, 7th, and 6th centuries are
remembered by the books which bear their names. They
exercised their difficult ministries in the midst of a divided
people, divided between the northern kingdom of Israel and

the southern kingdom of Judah, divided by a religious syncretism which tolerated the participation by many of the people in the fertility cult of the Canaanites, divided by shifting political alliances, and increasingly divided internally by the growing alienation between the affluent upper classes and the poor.

This final division on the basic of economic and social status was exacerbated by a corruption of those responsible for enforcing and interpreting Israel's law. It was the law itself, rooted in Israel's own experience of oppression in Egypt as we saw above, which was designed to insure justice and to protect the weak and the powerless. But a succession of grasping or ineffectual kings, dishonest judges, and weak elders so compromised the way justice was administered that the poor were left without protection from the greedy landlords and merchants. Worst of all, priests and people continued to piously practice a religion which, shorn of the law's insistence on justice and mercy, had become little more than empty ritual.

The prophets are not against cultic religion; it would be a mistake to so understand them. But they are clear in their understanding of the difference between true and false worship and unsparing of those who would substitute an empty cult for the acknowledgment owed the just and holy God of Israel.

Amos

One of the most outspoken in his condemnation of the dishonesty, greed, and lack of compassion of the upper classes was Amos. Originally from a small village called Tekoa not far from Jerusalem, Amos identifies himself as a shepherd. But from his skills as a breeder of sheep and a dresser of sycamore trees, it is more likely that he was a small landowner. Most of his prophetic ministry took place around the year 750 B.C. in the kingdom of Israel.

A careful reading of Amos brings out the differences between the prosperous and the poor. The former he accuses of storing up in their castles what they have extorted and stolen from the poor (3:10). They enjoy summer houses and spacious apartments ornamented with ivory (3:15). Their wives spend their time "lying upon beds of ivory," eating rich food, drinking wine, and listening to music (6:4-6). He is scathing on the subject of their lack of compassion and their oppression of the poor.

To the merchants with their dishonest business practices he says:

> Hear this, you who trample upon the needy
> and destroy the poor of the land!
> "When will the new moon be over," you ask
> "that we may sell our grain,
> and the sabbath, that we may display the wheat?
> We will diminish the ephah, add to the sheckel,
> and fix our scales for cheating!
> We will buy the lowly man for silver,
> and the poor man for a pair of sandals."
>
> Amos 8:4-6

To the dishonest judges, and to those who bribe them:

> Woe to those who turn judgment to wormwood
> and cast justice to the ground!
> They hate him who speaks the truth.
> Therefore, because you have trampled upon the weak
> and exacted of them levies of grain,
> though you have built houses of hewn stone,
> you shall not live in them!
> Yes, I know how many are your crimes,
> how grievous your sins:
> oppressing the just, accepting bribes,
> repelling the needy at the gate!
>
> Amos 5:7-12

What does Yahweh demand? Not religious celebrations and empty rituals, but a conversion of heart which will result in the restoration of justice:

> I hate, I spurn your feasts,
> I take no pleasure in your solemnities;
> Your cereal offerings I will not accept,
> nor consider your stall-fed peace offerings.

Away with your noisy songs!
I will not listen to the melodies of your harps.
But if you would offer me holocausts,
    then let justice surge like water,
    and goodness like an unfailing stream.

Amos 5:21-24

This criticism of external religiosity without a concern for justice and compassion towards the poor, both of which reflect an interior conversion of heart, is the hallmark of prophetic religion. It appears again in Isaiah, a prophet who appeared in Judah some ten or twenty years after Amos' ministry in Israel.

Isaiah

Born in Jerusalem, the city which was to remain the center of his prophetic ministry, Isaiah was probably of a noble family, judging from his easy access to the court. He may have been a priest. He received his call as a prophet around 742 B.C., the year that Uzziah died. Under Uzziah the little desert kingdom of Judah had become prosperous. Uzziah had repaired the defenses of Jerusalem, built up the army, improved the agriculture of his kingdom, extended its control over Edom and reopened the port at Ezion-geber on the Gulf of Aquabah. Trade was expanded and protected by a string of forts in the southern desert.

But with prosperity and affluence came the same social problems which for some time had plagued the northern kingdom of Israel. It was Isaiah's task to challenge the upper classes for their endless pursuit of wealth (3:16-24). He rebuked their princes, leading families, and corrupt judges for trampling on the rights of the poor (1:21-23; 5:23), grinding them down into poverty (3:13-15), stealing their land (5:8), exploiting the poor, the widows, and the orphans (10:2).

Like Amos, Isaiah is outraged at the pious religiosity of those who offer their gifts with the blood of their poor neighbors on their hands. This kind of religious observance is loathsome to Yahweh:

What care I for the number of your sacrifices?
says the Lord.

I have had enough of whole-burnt rams
and the fat of fatlings;
in the blood of calves, lambs and goats
I find no pleasure.
When you come in to visit me,
who asks these things of you?
Trample my courts no more!
Bring no more worthless offerings;
your incense is loathsome to me.
New moon and sabbath, calling of assemblies,
octaves with wickedness: these I cannot bear.
Your new moons and festivals I detest;
they weigh me down, I tire of the load.
When you spread out your hands,
I close my eyes to you;
Though you pray the more,
I will not listen.
Your hands are full of blood!
Wash yourselves clean!
Put away your misdeeds from before my eyes;
cease doing evil; learn to do good.
Make justice your aim: redress the wronged,
hear the orphan's plea, defend the widow.
                                    Isaiah 1:15-17

In the story of the vineyard which bore only wild grapes Isaiah told of Yahweh's disappointment with Israel and Judah: "He looked for justice, but behold, bloodshed; for righteousness, but behold, a cry" (5:7 RSV trans.).

Micah

Just as fierce a social critic was Isaiah's contemporary Micah. He denounced the wealthy landowners who were seizing the lands of the poor (2:1-2). The secular rulers who failed to uphold the law (3:1-3) and the religious leaders and judges who were guilty of selling their services or of taking bribes (3:11) also incurred his wrath. In a few words, Micah beautifully summed up prophetic religion: "You have been told ... what is good, and what the Lord requires of you: Only to do the right and to love goodness and to walk humbly with your God" (6:8).

Jeremiah

Fated to preach to Judah in the period prior to and during the fall of Jerusalem (587), Jeremiah is one of the most tragic figures in the Old Testament. Originally hopeful that Josiah's reform would lead to a genuine renewal and even the reunification of the two kingdoms, he gradually became convinced that a genuine conversion would not come about. Of a priestly family himself and deeply appreciative of Israel's religious tradition, he was forced to predict the loss of kingship, temple, ark, and priestly instruction. He painted a vivid picture of a people foolishly confident in what had become the official theology of the kingdom, God's promise to David in the Oracle of Nathan (2 Sam 7:8-16), while they continued to violate all terms of the covenant:

> Thus says the Lord of hosts, the God of Israel: Reform your ways and your deeds, so that I may remain with you in this place. Put not your trust in the deceitful words: "This is the temple of the Lord! The temple of the Lord! The temple of the Lord!" Only if you thoroughly reform your ways and your deeds; if each of you deals justly with his neighbor; if you no longer oppress the resident alien, the orphan, and the widow; if you no longer shed innocent blood in this place, or follow strange gods to your own harm, will I remain with you in this place, in the land which I gave your fathers long ago and forever.
>
> Jeremiah 7:3-7

Trito-Isaiah

A final passage, generally thought to have been written after the exile by a disciple of Deutero-Isaiah, concerns the ancient practice of fasting. In insisting that fasting and other penitential practices are useless, if not combined with a concern for justice and the needs of the poor, this dialogue between God and the people is very much in the prophetic tradition.

> "Why do we fast, and you do not see it?
> afflict ourselves, and you take no note of it?"
> Lo, on your fast day you carry out your own pursuits,

and drive all your laborers.
Yes, your fast ends in quarreling and fighting,
striking with wicked claw.
Would that today you might fast
so as to make your voice heard on high!
Is this the manner of fasting I wish,
of keeping a day of penance;
that a man bow his head like a reed,
and lie in sackcloth and ashes?
Do you call this a fast,
a day acceptable to the Lord?
This, rather, is the fasting that I wish:
releasing those bound unjustly,
untying the thongs of the yoke;
setting free the oppressed,
breaking every yoke;
sharing your bread with the hungry,
sheltering the oppressed and the homeless;
clothing the naked when you see them,
and not turning your back on your own.

> Isaiah 58:3-7

The parallels between this passage, read in the liturgy of the church at the beginning of the season of Lent, and the preaching of Jesus should not be surprising, for Jesus himself comes out of this prophetic tradition.

The Social Dimensions of the Gospel

From the beginning there is a strong social dimension to Jesus preaching. First, that Gospel is good news for the poor. Second, Jesus calls others to discipleship in the service of God's reign, a discipleship which is inclusive of every dimension of human life, social, sexual, and economic. Thus we will consider Jesus' critical attitude towards wealth and the self-sacrificial love he taught. Finally, we will consider the para-doxical reversal so often expressed in his preaching; in the reign of God the first become last and the last first.

1. Good News for the Poor

Luke represents Jesus at the very beginning of his ministry announcing the coming of the messianic age with a quote from the prophet Isaiah; the time of fulfillment means specifically good news for the poor (Isa 61:1-2):

> The Spirit of the Lord is upon me;
> because he has anointed me
> to bring glad tidings to the poor.
> He has sent me to proclaim liberty to captives
> and recovery of sight to the blind,
> to let the oppressed go free,
> and to proclaim a year acceptable to the Lord.
>
> Luke 4:18-19

Jesus' term for this messianic fulfillment is the kingdom of God (Mk 1:15). The coming of God's kingdom or reign is the theme that dominates the preaching of Jesus, but nowhere more so than in what is generally referred to as the Sermon on the Mount (Matt 5:1-7:27), though in Luke, this great sermon of Jesus takes place on a plain (Lk 6:20-49).

The Beatitudes. The material presented by the two evangelists represents typical sayings of Jesus collected in the Q source into the sermon. Because of the similarities between the two accounts many commentators conclude that both versions reflect a sermon of Jesus containing the beatitudes and a number of specific instructions defining the response of the disciples in terms of love of neighbor.[12]

MATTHEW 5:3-12	LUKE 6:20-26
Blessed are the poor in spirit, for theirs is the kingdom of heaven.	Blessed are you poor, for the kingdom of God is yours.
Blessed are they who mourn, for they will be comforted.	Blessed are you who are now hungry, for you will be satisfied.
[Blessed are the meek, for they will inherit the land.]	Blessed are you who are now weeping, for you will laugh.

Blessed are those who hunger and thirst for righteousness, for they will be satisfied.

[Blessed are the merciful, for they will be shown mercy.

Blessed are the clean of heart, for they will see God.

Blessed are the peacemakers, for they will be called children of God.

Blessed are they who are persecuted for the sake of righteousness, for theirs is the kingdom of heaven.]

Blessed are you when they insult you and persecute you and utter every kind of evil against you [falsely] because of me. Rejoice and be glad, for your reward will be great in heaven Thus they persecuted the prophets who were before you.

Blessed are you when people hate you, and when they exclude and insult you and denounce your name as evil, on account of the Son Man.

Rejoice and leap for joy on that day! Behold, your reward will be great in heaven. For their ancestors treated the prophets in the same way.

[But woe to you who are rich, for you have received your consolation.

But woe to you who are filled now, for you will be hungry.

Woe to you who laugh now, for you will grieve and weep.

Woe to you when all speak well of you, for their ancestors treated the false prophets in this way.]

In teaching God's special concern for the poor and the powerless, the beatitudes reflect the prophetic tradition. Luke's version of the beatitudes is shorter than Matthew's and thought to be closer to the original. However both evangelists seem to have adapted the received tradition and added some verses of their own composition (given here in brackets).

Luke's version appears at first glance more radical than Matthew's, but the prophetic concern for the oppressed and the powerless is present in both evangelists. Matthew's "poor in spirit" should be understood in the Old Testament sense of the *anawim,* the poor of Yahweh. Originally this term referred to those who were actually poor, but it came to be used of those without material resources or power, the poor, the sick, the widows and orphans who could look only to God for their well-being and deliverance.[13] It does not mean the comfortable who maintain an interior detachment from their wealth. Similarly, Matthew 5:6 is usually translated as those who hunger and thirst for "righteousness." But as John Topel points out, behind the Greek *dikaiosyne* (justice, righteousness) lies the Hebrew *sedek* which most often means the justice which expresses one's righteousness before God. "Thus the primary meaning here: seeking justice means to be holy."[14]

In both versions of Jesus' sermon the beatitudes describe those who will find fulfillment in the kingdom of God, though Luke emphasizes that those called blest find fulfillment even now. Matthew makes entrance into the kingdom dependent on one's conduct towards others, particularly towards the poor and unfortunate, in his parable of the Last Judgment:

> Then he will say to those on his left: 'Depart from me, you accursed, into the eternal fire prepared for the devil and his angels. For I was hungry and you gave me no food, I was thirsty and you gave me no drink, a stranger and you gave me no welcome, naked and you gave me no clothing, ill and in prison, and you did not care for me.'
>
> Matthew 25:41-44

2. The Call to Discipleship

Jesus did not come to found a religion. He called all who would listen to discipleship with him in the service of the Kingdom of God. The New Testament uses the Greek word for disciple, *mathētēs,* about 250 times. In the gospels discipleship includes every dimension of human life; it shapes one's attitude towards property and wealth, effects a person's human and erotic relationships, gives a new meaning to love, and finally, changes the way one understands success and personal fulfillment.

The call to discipleship is expressed in many ways. One of

the most radical statements occurs in the story of the rich young man. To this man, who has kept all the commandments since his youth, Jesus says: "You are lacking in one thing. Go, sell what you have, and give to the poor and you will have treasure in heaven; then come, follow me" (Mk 10:21). Discipleship means a clean break with the past (Lk 9:57-60). Those who followed Jesus "left everything" (Lk 5:11); they left behind jobs (Mk 2:14), parents, family, and children (Lk 14:26). For some, it also meant celibacy for the sake of the kingdom (Matt 19:11-12). Discipleship involved an *imitatio Christi;* those who followed Jesus were called to take up the cross and even to be willing to give up their own lives (Mk 8:34-35; John 15:13).

Disciples also shared in Jesus' ministry, for unlike the Pharisees, Jesus sent his disciples out to teach and act in his name (Matt 10:5ff; Lk 10:1ff). Their attitude towards authority was to be respectful but not uncritical (Mk 12:17; Matt 23:2-3). He warned them that they would be rejected by others, persecuted by religious and civil authorities, even alienated from their own families (Matt 10).

The gospel of Mark provides an extended instruction on the nature of discipleship in a section sometimes referred to as "the Way of the Son of Man" (Mk 8:27-10:52). Several times the section mentions that Jesus and his disciples were "on the way" (Mk 8:27; 9:33; 10:32, 52). Structurally, the section contains three predictions of the passion; each is followed by a misunderstanding on the part of the disciples and an instruction by Jesus on the nature of discipleship.

First, Peter tries to talk Jesus out of his coming passion; Jesus responds by saying, "Whoever wishes to come after me must deny himself, take up his cross, and follow me" (Mk 8:34).

After the second prediction of the passion, an argument breaks out among the disciples over who is the most important. Jesus responds by saying, "If anyone wishes to be first, he shall be the last of all and the servant of all" (Mk 9:35).

Finally, immediately after the third prediction, James and John approach him and ask to sit at his right and left hand in glory. Jesus again says, "whoever wishes to be great among you will be your servant; whoever wishes to be first among you will be the slave of all. For the Son of Man did not come to be served but to serve and to give his life as a ransom for many" (Mk 10:43-45). Thus discipleship, if modeled on the example of Jesus, means a denial of self and a willingness to be at the service of others. The entire section is bracketed by two different stories in which Jesus cures a blind man, perhaps to symbolize that he alone can open the eyes of the disciples who seem so unable to understand his teaching.

3. Critical Attitude Towards Wealth

Jesus' attitude towards wealth is frequently a critical one. In the story of the young man who turns away from Jesus' call to discipleship because of his many possessions he says, "how hard it is to enter the kingdom of God! It is easier for a camel to pass through the eye of a needle than for one who is rich to enter the kingdom of God" (Mk 10:24-25). Jesus seems to see wealth as an obstacle; it too easily becomes an end in itself, leading to a comfortable existence which can close one off from the call to discipleship. It can also blind one to the needs of others, leading to exclusion from the kingdom.

The parable of the fool who grows rich for himself rather than rich in the sight of God (Lk 12:16-21) and the story of the rich man who allowed Lazarus to starve at his gate (Lk 16:19-31) underline the danger of riches. The response of the wealthy tax collector Zacchaeus illustrates concretely what conversion to Jesus' message means: "Behold, half of my possessions, Lord, I shall give to the poor, and if I have extorted anything from anyone I shall repay it four times over" (Lk 19:8).

Jesus did not demand a complete renunciation of property of all who followed him; indeed he seems to have had friends who were able to provide hospitality and support for him and his disciples. Nevertheless he frequently warns against the danger of riches and calls his disciples to an evangelical simplicity (Mk 6:8-9). Disciples should be willing to share whatever they have: "Give to everyone who asks of you ... lend expecting nothing back" (Lk 6:30, 35).

4. Self-Sacrificial Love

What kind of love does Jesus ask of his disciples? When

asked which is the greatest commandment, Jesus links love of God and love of neighbor (Mk 12:28-31). He calls his disciples to be reconciled with one another before taking part in divine worship (Matt 5:32-24). They are also called to reconcile others; the term "peacemakers" in Matthew's version of the beatitudes refers to those who reconcile quarrels. The parable of the good Samaritan (Lk 10:29-37) makes it clear that no one is to be excluded from the category of neighbor.

Throughout his preaching Jesus urges his disciples to love even their enemies, or more accurately, as Leonardo Boff points out: "There are no more friends or enemies, neighbors or strangers. There are only brothers and sisters."[15] Jesus insists that his disciples model their love on the all inclusive love of God:

> You have heard that it was said, 'You shall love your neighbor and hate your enemy.' But I say to you, love your enemies, and pray for those who persecute you, that you may be children of your heavenly Father, for he makes his sun rise on the bad and the good, and causes rain to fall on the just and the unjust. For if you love those who love you, what recompense will you have? Do not the tax collectors do the same. And if you greet your brothers only, what is unusual about that? Do not the pagans do the same? So be perfect, just as your heavenly Father is perfect.
>
> Matt 5:43-48

Luke especially emphasizes the inclusive love of Jesus in his words and even more in his actions. He shows Jesus' special concern for marginalized groups, women, Samaritans, lepers, public sinners, and especially the poor.

Jesus seems to reject the traditional principle of retaliation, returning violence for violence. Instead he instructs his disciples to place others first; they should yield to them and be willing to bear even insult and injury. Some have seen in the command to turn the other cheek a demand for absolute non-violence. Jesus also rules out resorting to litigation in defense of one's personal rights or property (as does Paul in 1 Corinthians 6:1-7). He urges his disciples to go along with even unreasonable requests, and to accommodate those who ask for gifts or

loans: The following few verses are among the most difficult
and challenging in the Gospel:

> You have heard that it was said, 'An eye for an eye and a
> tooth for a tooth.' But I say to you, offer no resistance to
> one who is evil. When someone strikes you on your right
> cheek, turn the other one to him as well. If anyone wants to
> go to law with you over your tunic, hand him your cloak as
> well. Should anyone press you into service for one mile, go
> with him for two miles. Give to the one who asks of you,
> and do not turn your back on one who wants to borrow.
>
> Matt 5:38-42

How can these sayings be explained? Most Christians would
acknowledge that they find it difficult to practice the values
expressed in the Sermon on the Mount in their own lives.
Even more, the values of the sermon call into question many
institutions and structures taken for granted by modern
nations. The efforts of the medieval church to forbid usury,
the practice of lending money at interest, is only one example
of an ultimately unsuccessful attempt to structure into civic life
what was understood to be a Gospel demand.[16] For Martin
Luther, what Jesus called for was simply beyond what sinful
human beings like ourselves could realize, and so the Sermon
on the Mount becomes a revelation of our own radical sin-
fulness.

But Jesus is proclaiming neither an impossible ideal nor an
elitist ethic for the few. He is not a utopian dreamer, but one
who calls his disciples to a profound conversion here and now,
in this world. They are to put their own rights aside so that
they might place the needs of others first. The Gospel remains
a challenge which continues to call our own lives and our
societies into question.

But Jesus goes even further. He reminds his disciples that he
came "not to be served but to serve and to give his life as a
ransom for many" (Mk 10:45). They are to follow his example.
Christian discipleship means self-denial, service of others, even
the willingness to give up one's life. Thus it requires a self-
sacrificial love. Perhaps this is nowhere more clearly expressed
than in John, where Jesus says: "This is my commandment:

love one another as I love you. No has has greater love than this, to lay down one's life for one's friends" (John 15:12-13).

5. *The Last Shall Be First*

In Luke's sermon on the plain, the blessings directed towards the poor, the hungry, and the sorrowful are followed by the "woes" or curses, directed towards the comfortable and the affluent who remain unconverted (Lk 6:24-26). Here is the "eschatological reversal" so present in the Jesus tradition, the promise of the kingdom to the poor, the wounded, and the marginalized which often means that the first become last and the last become first (Mk 10:31). God has thrown down rulers from their thrones but lifted up the lowly. The hungry God has filled with good things and sent the rich away empty (Lk 1:52-53; cf. 16:25).[17]

For the disciples of Jesus, this eschatological reversal turns the normal meaning of success and fulfillment upside down. Fulfillment in the reign of God cannot be measured by worldly standards. In some paradoxical way, self-fulfillment comes only through a self-emptying on behalf of others. In Mark Jesus says, "Whoever wishes to save his life will lose it, but whoever loses his life for my sake and that of the gospel will save it" (Mk 8:35). His saying about the last being first and the first last occurs in the context of those disciples who have left everything to follow him (Mk 10:29-31).

Conclusion

The Gospel Jesus proclaimed summoned men and women to discipleship in the service of God's reign. That discipleship did not involve an otherworldly asceticism. Hans Küng has emphasized that Jesus was not a monk or ascetic who counseled separation from the world, like the Essenes at Qumran. His message was addressed to all people, not just to an elite.[18] He did not proclaim a higher perfection or ethic for the disciples, for the chosen few. The universality of his message can be seen from the fact that it was precisely in the world that the disciples of Jesus were to be involved.

Yet the Gospel itself is radical, even revolutionary. Rooted in the prophetic tradition of Israel, with its profound sense of God's justice and concern for the poor, it calls all who have ears to hear to a radically new vision and a new way of living. Its emphasis on self-sacrificial love stands as a direct challenge to contemporary western culture which celebrates self-fulfillment and personal autonomy and emphasizes individual freedom at the expense of the common good.

The reign of God is inclusive of all dimensions of human life. Those who live as disciples of Jesus, seeking God's reign through prayer and compassionate service, reproducing in their own lives his self-sacrificial love, enable others to recognize God's presence and action in the world. They become living signs of God's presence until he comes again.

It would be a mistake to so idealize Jesus' call to discipleship that it would be placed beyond the realm of possibility for the ordinary believer. Such an elitism would itself be contrary to the Gospel. As Andrew Greeley has argued in recent years, God is present and disclosed to us "in the grace-full persons, events and objects of daily, secular life."[19] Human intimacy and marital love, the birth of a child, personal struggle and renewal, reconciliation, a meal or family celebration, an experience of community—all can be sacramental moments which disclose God's active presence at the very center of human life. Discipleship can never exclude these profound human realities.

On the other hand, responding to Jesus' call to discipleship is never without cost,[20] whether it is lived out in contemplative solitude, as a dedicated single person, a spouse or family member, or as a member of a radical Christian community.

Though these Christian communities are only one response to the call to discipleship, they have appeared in every age of the church. They represent the attempt of men and women to root their own lives in the person and message of Jesus. Many have taken their inspiration from Jesus' invitation to the rich young man: "Go, sell what you have and give to the poor . . . then come, follow me" (Mk 10:21). In the following chapters we will consider some of the forms that these radical Christian communities have taken.

2

The Monastic Movement

Shortly after the Second World War broke upon the United States at Pearl Harbor, a young man with hopes of being a writer left the college where he was teaching in New York and presented himself at the gate of the monastery of Gethsemani in Kentucky, asking for admission. Gethsemani was a Trappist community; it belonged to a monastic order whose name was synonymous with austerity.

The man, Thomas Merton, had visited the monastery once before and had been struggling for some time with the question of whether or not he should enter the community. He was attracted to the life and the complete offering of self that it represented, but feared that his own past, prior to his conversion, might prevent him from being accepted. In *The Seven Storey Mountain,* one of the classics of contemporary religious autobiography, he tells how he came to his decision. Wandering the campus one evening he made a desperate prayer:

> Suddenly, as soon as I had made that prayer, I became aware of the wood, the trees, the dark hills, the wet night wind, and then, clearer than any of these obvious realities, in my imagination, I started to hear the great bell of Gethsemani ringing in the night—the bell in the big gray tower, ringing and ringing, as if it were just behind the first hill. The impression made me breathless, and I had to think twice to realize that it was only in my imagination that I was hearing the bell of the Trappist Abbey ringing in the

dark. Yet, as I afterwards calculated, it was just about that
time that the bell is rung every night for the *Salve Regina,*
towards the end of Compline.

The bell seemed to be telling me where I belonged—as if
it were calling me home.[1]

After consulting one of the priests at the college, Merton
went to Gethsemani and was accepted. He thought that he
had left his career as a writer behind, but the story of his
conversion and monastic vocation, brilliantly told in his 1948
autobiography, was to bring him an international reputation.
A flood of books and articles followed. Merton's career was
cut short by his tragic death in Thailand in 1968. But his
works in the intervening years revealed his growth as he
wrestled in solitude with God and his own restless spirit. Over
the years his interests broadened, turning ultimately to issues
troubling the world beyond the monastery gate, racism, the
war in Vietnam, oppression, violence, the specter of a nuclear
holocaust. His interest in the religious traditions of the East
continued to deepen. Addressing these issues was for Merton
as much part of a contemplative life as was his earlier writing
on monasticism and prayer. As his books were republished
and translated into other languages, Merton himself became a
symbol of the enduring meaning of a monastic life deeply
rooted in the history of the church.

Anthony

The man universally recognized as the father of Christian
monasticism was a third century Egyptian hermit by the name
of Anthony. His biography, the *Life of Anthony* written by St.
Athanasius (297-373), was an early example of the long tradition of Christian hagiography, the idealized biography of
some one considered a saint. It was to have a profound impact
on the Christianity of both the East and the West.

Anthony was born about the year 250, of affluent parents
who died when he was about twenty years old, leaving him
with an estate and a younger sister to care for. According to
his biographer, his inherited wealth lay heavily on his mind.
He thought frequently of the story of the early Christians who,
according to the Acts of the Apostles (4:34-35), sold their

property and handed the proceeds over to the apostles to care for the needs of the poor. Then about six months after the death of his parents Anthony had an experience which was to change his life. He had gone into a church:

> It happened that the Gospel was then being read, and he heard the Lord saying to the rich man: "If thou wilt be perfect, go, sell what thou hast, and give to the poor, and thou shalt have treasure in heaven; and come, follow me." As though God had inspired his thought of the saints and the passage had been read aloud on his account, Anthony left the church at once and gave to the villagers the property he had received from his parents—there were three hundred acres, fertile and very beautiful—so that he and his sister might not be in any way encumbered by it. He sold all their other worldly possessions and collected a large amount of money, which he gave to the poor, keeping a little for his sister's sake.[2]

Anthony's experience in the church—like Merton's experience of hearing the bells of Gethsemani in his imagination—is a classic literary example of a graced moment in which a call to a new way of living the Christian life is discerned. In traditional language, he had recognized his vocation.

Anthony was quick to respond. After disposing of his possessions he found a place to stay on the outskirts of the village and began to live as a hermit. An older man living a solitary life in a neighboring village served as an example for Anthony, and he sought out others from whom he might learn about the spiritual life. For a while he lived in some old tombs at some distance from the village. Later he withdrew deeper into the desert where he lived in the ruins of an ancient fort not far from the coast of the Red Sea. For twenty years he lived as a hermit, devoting himself to prayer and an ascetical discipline of fasts and vigils.

As his reputation grew, others began to follow his example and to seek out his advice; a number became his disciples, settling near him to pursue the eremetical, or hermit, life in their huts or "cells" under his direction. They were called "monks," from the Greek *monos,* which means alone. Anthony was not the first of these hermit monks, but the immense popularity of his *Life,* written in 356 shortly after his death, was to lead countless others to seek God in the desert. Besides circulating widely in several languages in the East, it was translated almost immediately into Latin and within twenty years was being read in the West.

The Call of the Desert

The desert has always been a rich symbol in religious literature. The word desert suggest spaciousness, dryness, and solitude. It is a barren place, isolated and unforgiving, exposed to the elemental forces which beat down upon the unprotected earth. The desert is a hostile environment, but there is also a profound peace in the desert which can quiet and center those who venture into its solitude. In the Bible the desert is the place for the encounter with God. Stripped of distractions and open to the infinite mystery of the universe sensed in the sun, the wind, the alternating heat and cold, and the vast expanse of the stars, the man or woman in the desert stands naked and alone before God's mysterious presence.

However one cannot encounter God without also coming face to face with one's self (cf. Lk 5:8), and so the desert is also an arena for the struggle with the evil spirits, the demonic powers which contend for control of the human spirit. According to the synoptic gospels, Jesus withdrew after his baptism into the desert where he was tempted by the devil. It was only after this period of personal struggle that he began his own public ministry. Similarly, the *Life of Anthony* is full of vivid stories of his struggle with the devil who sought to turn him from his purpose by appearing under various disguises or by filling his imagination with sensual images and arousing in him sexual feelings. Thus the desert can be also a place of testing and purification.

What led so many Christians in the third and fourth centuries to leave the cities and withdraw into the desert? Partly this was due to the example of Anthony and the great success of his *Life.* But there were other reasons as well.

In the East there was a rural dimension to the monastic

movement from the beginning. From its earliest days Christianity had been largely an urban religion. It is not surprising that the two great missionary apostles, Peter and Paul, both made their way to the capital city of the Empire, Rome. But as Christianity spread into the interiors of Egypt and Syria, beyond the extension of the Hellenistic culture of their cities, it began to take root in a peasantry who preferred to live as far away as possible from the imperial officials and tax collectors of the cities. These officials were beginning to extend their authority over the villages of Egypt about the time that Anthony withdrew to the desert. Some went to the desert to seek a more simple life. Others had been driven there by persecution. Thus the initial growth of monasticism in the East was not unrelated to various social changes and pressures.

Another important factor was the establishment of the church which followed shortly after the peace of Constantine (313), allowing Christians religious freedom. Prior to this time occasional persecutions and the lack of public recognition meant that Christianity was still a counter-cultural movement, the practice of which entailed considerable sacrifice and occasionally martyrdom. But with the passing of the age of martyrs Christianity became not only acceptable but respectable as well. The church, anxious not to jeopardize its newly found acceptance, was not particularly interested in challenging the social stratification of society. For many, being a good Christian meant little more than being a good citizen. Others, sensing the direction in which the new winds were blowing, sought baptism as a way of social advancement.

Thus the challenge was diminishing. Christian life was less and less understood as a Gospel call to discipleship. For many it was understood in terms of the practice and observances of a religion which was fast becoming the official cult of the empire. And as the church began to appropriate for its officials the empire's symbols of authority and power, it became itself more worldly. Christianity was becoming increasingly conformed to the world in which it found itself.

It is important to note that the monastic movement was in its beginnings largely a movement of lay people. Many Christians who had understood their faith as a protest against the hedonism and immorality of Roman culture now found themselves protesting as well against the increasing worldliness of the church. Some authors stress that the monastic movement was as much a reaction to the growing clericalism and sacerdotalism of the church as it was a desire to flee the corruption of the cities.[3] Many men and women felt that something had gone wrong, that the Gospel call to renunciation, sacrifice, and holiness had fallen on deaf ears. At the same time, the example of the martyrs continued to inspire those who sought to live out the Gospel in its fullness. The example of those who left the cities for the desert to discipline their flesh and struggle against the demons suggested a new kind of martyrdom. In the early monastic literature the image of this new "white" or bloodless martyrdom appears frequently.

Finally, the idealism present in the Gospel itself should not be overlooked. Jesus challenges his disciples to deny themselves, take up the cross, and follow him (Mk 8:34); he called them "to be perfect, just as your heavenly Father is perfect" (Matt 5:48) and praised those who had given up "houses or brothers or sisters or mother or father or children or lands" for his sake (Mk 10:29). The ideal of celibacy is present in Jesus' words about those who have renounced marriage for the sake of the kingdom of heaven (Matt 19:12).

What then was it that those who joined this movement into the desert were seeking? First of all, like Anthony, they sought to respond fully to the call of Christ to a radical discipleship by disposing of their possessions and leaving behind not just their worldly concerns but their relatives and friends as well. Following these evangelical "counsels," they chose a radically simple "lifestyle" of prayer and manual labor; simple food, plain dress, and basic shelter was to become the norm. From their renunciation of possessions and marriage and their willingness to submit themselves to another for spiritual direction came ultimately the religious vows of poverty, chastity, and obedience.

Secondly, they sought to discipline their bodies and conquer their sensual appetites through fasting, vigils, penances, and other "ascetical" exercises. The Greek word *askesis* was used for athletic exercise, and so these solitaries or "monks" were often referred to as ascetics. Some of them went to extremes of penance and self-discipline that reflected more a gnostic disdain for the body than a Christian sense for its holiness. Probably the most famous example is Simeon the Stylite (390-459), so called because he lived for thirty-seven years atop a narrow column raised some sixty feet above the desert floor. Many of these solitaries were dirty and unkempt. Jerome claims to have seen an ascetic who lived for thirty years on barley bread and muddy water and another whose daily meal consisted of five dates.[4] But for many, ascetical discipline was practiced as a preparation for a life of prayer.

Most of all, they sought through their renunciation, ascetical practices, and prayer that union with God which to this day constitutes the goal of the monastic life.

Hermits and Cenobites in the East

The monastic movement began in the East, primarily in the desert hinterlands of Egypt, Syria, and Palestine. Many of these first monks were hermits; their life was described as eremitical, from the Greek *eremos* which meant a deserted place or desert. There were thousands of hermits living in the desert by the time of Anthony's death. Often they lived in colonies grouped around a few common buildings. Such a colony was called a *làura.* It was not really a community in the later monastic sense, for the life of the monks was extremely independent. Most of the time they remained alone in their cells, praying and weaving the baskets and mats out of reeds which they sold to support themselves. They would gather perhaps once a week for the Eucharist and prayer. An older member served as a spiritual guide or director; he was called *abbas,* or father, from which comes the word abbot.

Pachomius

Monastic community life was given its first form and direction by the monk Pachomius (c. 292-346), a contemporary of Anthony. Conscripted into the Roman army in his youth, Pachomius retained a soldier's sense for discipline. After his military service he became a Christian and then a hermit, but soon was led to organize a community of monks in the upper Nile valley at Tabennesis in Egypt.

In this community the monks followed a common life. Though each monk had a private cell, they lived together in common houses or buildings, each under the direction of an appointed leader. Obedience to this leader or superior was added to the poverty and chastity already observed by the monks.[5] They ate together, held their goods in common, and followed a common order of communal prayer, manual labor, and later study. Before long candidates were required to undergo a probationary period, later known as the novitiate, before being fully accepted into the community. This way of life was called cenobitic, from the Greek *koinos bios,* common life.

So successful was Pachomius' organization of the monastic impulse that within a few years he had more than three thousand followers. By the time of his death in 346 he had established a number of communities for men and one for women. Each monastery was a large complex consisting of a group of houses, a church and some common buildings, all surrounded by a wall or enclosure. After his death his successors published a text or *Rules,* based at least in part on his writings. Through Jerome's translation it became known in the West.

Basil

While many of the early ascetics were lacking in formal education, Basil of Caesarea (c. 330-379) had studied in both Constantinople and Athens. Though he was attracted to the monastic life and had established a community of monks at his home in Pontus in Asia Minor, his talents were such that he was not able to pursue for long a life of solitude himself. Elected bishop of Caesarea, he was involved in the struggle against Arianism. But his contributions to the monastic movement were considerable.

One of his greatest achievements was to secure monasticism firmly within the church. The early ascetics had been mostly lay people, inspired at least in part by a dissatisfaction with the growing worldliness of the church. The monastic movement developed apart from the church, away from the jurisdiction of its bishops and at times without the help of its sacraments.

Anthony went for years without participating in the liturgy or the sacraments. A community usually had a few priests to celebrate the liturgy, but the clericalization of the monastic order was still several centuries away. Had a monastic priesthood developed in this early period, it might have further isolated the movement from the church.[6]

Related to the independence of the monastic movement was its tendency towards an extreme individualism. The monastic ideal was a call to perfection or holiness which was completely open to all Christians. Yet with its emphasis on renunciation, self-denial, and personal perfection, all strengthened by the dualism of the Hellenistic culture, it was open to distortion and even fanaticism. Simeon on his pillar hardly provides a fitting model of the Christian life. Many ascetics attempted to outdo each other in the severity of their penances.

As a bishop who had been first a monk, Basil was successful in tempering this fierce spirit of competition through his *Rules* which put equal emphasis on the law of charity and the works of mercy. To combat self-will and the pride that can so easily result, he stressed the importance of monastic obedience. He urged that monasteries be located closer to the cities and that they find ways to care for the sick and the poor, offer hospitality to travelers, and instruction for others. In this way Basil helped to integrate what could have easily become a separate movement into the wider community of the church. His *Rules* remains the basis of the monastic life in the Orthodox churches to this day.

Evagrius

One early monastic theologian and writer, Evagrius of Pontus (346-399), was to have a significant impact on the development of monastic spirituality even though his thought was condemned at the Fifth Ecumenical Council (553) for its Origenism. Evagrius, influenced by neo-Platonic philosophy, focused on the mind. He divided the spiritual life into two distinct stages, the "active" life concerned with the purification of the senses and the acquisition of virtue, and the "contemplative" life through which the mind, once quieted and emptied of distractions, might be united with God. Evagrius' mystical theology has been described as "Origen de-Christianized."[7]

Others would more adequately address the place of the heart in spirituality and stress the christological and pneumatological dimensions of a theology of prayer. But his systematization, with its emphasis on contemplation, was to play a major role in the development of spirituality in both the East and the West.

Monasticism in the West

Rome had its own ascetics, living either in their family homes or in informal groups, before the beginning of the fourth century. But enthusiasm for the monastic movement began to grow as the growing monastic literature and the personal reports brought by travelers, returning pilgrims, and occasionally, ecclesiastical refugees, began reaching the West in the fourth century. Athanasius, the patriarch of Alexandra, brought news of the ascetics of the East to Rome shortly after being exiled from his See in 339. Jerome arrived in Rome in 383 after spending two years as a rather active hermit in Syria. He spent several years there before returning to the East in 385 for good, settling in Bethlehem. Jerome did much to popularize both the monastic life and the misguided notion that virginity is a superior state to marriage.

Women played a considerable role in the development of asceticism in the West. At Rome in the fourth century a group of aristocratic women followed an asceticism of prayer, fasting, simple lifestyle, and charitable works even before Jerome's arrival.[8] Melania the Elder, a wealthy Roman woman, moved to Jerusalem around 378 where she governed a community of some fifty women on the Mount of Olives. A number of women, strongly influenced by Jerome, who became their director, practiced celibacy and gave themselves to the study of scripture. In 386 two of Jerome's friends, Paula and Eustochium, after a pilgrimage to Jerusalem and a visit to the monastic communities in the Nile valley, settled in Bethlehem in their own monastery near Jerome's.

Ambrose established an order of virgins or religious women in Milan. Though they continued to live with their parents, they took public vows of virginity and had a special place reserved for them in the church. Thus the flight to the desert was not the only kind of asceticism; many women and men lived a kind of urban monasticism. Rather than an institution, the monastic movement represented primarily the choice of a Gospel lifestyle. In one of his letters Jerome praises Pammachius, a Roman senator who after the death of his wife embraced the monastic life, renouncing the affluence to which he had been accustomed, spending his time and fortune on the poor and sick of Rome, even wearing the somber garb of a monk into the senate.[9] For women particularly, the monastic life provided an alternative to marriage and offered them a new independence from the roles dictated by their culture.

By 384, some twenty years after it appeared in the East, a Latin version of the *Life of Anthony* was being read at Rome, Milan, and Trier. It was to have a great impact, but was only one example of an new ascetical literature. Much of it was based on the translation of eastern works.[10]

But the western church was also beginning to produce its own monastic writers and founders. Augustine attributes his own conversion in 386 to the extraordinary impact of the *Life of Anthony* on the friends of a friend who told him the story.[11] Augustine began himself to live an ascetical life, and before long had established a number of monasteries which spread the monastic life through North Africa. After becoming Bishop of Hippo in 396 he organized his own clergy into a community; they shared their possessions, took their meals in common, and lived simply. From the letter he wrote to a community of nuns in Hippo was to come his Rule, which came to be used by the Canons of St. Augustine in the eleventh century, the Dominicans in the thirteenth, as well as a considerable number of communities today.

Monasticism was to find especially fertile soil in France. In the earliest period three names stand out. Martin of Tours (317-397) planted the monastic life at Marmoutier in central Gaul about 360; he ultimately became bishop of Tours. In the South, Honoratus established a community in 395 on the island of Lerins (now St. Honorat) off the coast of Cannes. John Cassian, a monk originally from Bethlehem, had become familiar with the theology of Evagrius of Pontus while living in Egypt. He came to Gaul and settled at Marseilles around

415 where he founded a monastery for men and another for women. His *Institutions* and *Conferences* were to become classics of western monastic theology. The monasticism which developed in Gaul from these various sources was to be later transformed through the impact of the rule of Benedict, but not before its own monastic missionaries had brought the monastic movement to the British Isles, particularly, to Ireland.

Celtic Monasticism

Christianity may have come to Britain as early as the third century. There seem to have been bishops at London and York by the time the Emperor Constantine accepted the faith (312). But as the Roman troops were withdrawn towards the end of the fourth century and the southern part of Britain was invaded by the pagan Anglo-Saxons, the church there suffered great losses.

In Ireland, Christianity and the name of St. Patrick are inseparably intertwined, but there were already some Christians in Ireland when Patrick arrived in 432.[12] Patrick himself, most probably born in England, had been kidnapped by Irish raiders and brought to Ireland to work as a slave. Some six years later he escaped, leaving Ireland on a ship which brought him to Gaul. He spent the better part of the next twenty years there, learning in his wanderings about the monastic life. Most important in his monastic education was the time spent on the island of Lerins with Honoratus and his community. Thus the Christianity he brought to Ireland when he returned there as a missionary bishop was heavily influenced by the monasticism he had become familiar with in Gaul.

Once planted, monasticism quickly spread throughout Ireland. St. Brigid established a "double" monastery of men and women at Kildare in the fifth century. In the sixth, monastic communities were founded at Clonmacnoise, Clonfert, and Durrow in the center, Derry and Bangor in the North, and at Glendalough in the Southeast. Celtic monasticism was present also in Wales and later in Scotland.

Though Patrick seems to have brought the episcopal office to Ireland along with monastic life, it was monasticism which for centuries was to play the dominant role in the Irish church.

Irish culture was rural and tribal, rather than urban; it did not lend support to a strong episcopacy. But the central role of the clan in early Irish history was to give a uniquely Irish stamp to the monasticism which flourished there.[13] While some monastic foundations were exclusively for ascetics and contemplatives, many were family or clan communities in which ascetics lived in close proximity with lay families and their children. Not all monks were celibate; some, called *manaig,* were lay monks who were married and worked as farmers.

Each monastery was generally enclosed by an outer wall made of earth and stone. Inside were the cultivated fields, outbuildings, and huts. At the center was the church, often several of them, the cemetery, the cells of the monks, frequently resembling beehives, and some communal buildings, among them a refectory, the round tower which even today symbolizes Celtic monasteries, a guest house, and often a school. The buildings were usually made of wood. The central area was surrounded by another wall, forming an inner enclosure, while the ascetics frequently had their own area within it separated off from the rest of the community. These monastic settlements provided pastoral care for those who lived in the surrounding villages and became centers of learning, known for their libraries and their art.

The monasteries were led by abbots, priest-monks who were generally clan leaders. Sometimes they were bishops as well, but more often their power was greater than that of the bishop who might also live within the community to provide the necessary sacramental ministry. Thus the real church leadership in Ireland was that of the monastic abbots. Only in the twelfth century did Ireland begin to adopt the diocesan structures and forms of religious community which characterized the rest of the western church.

Irish monks were famous as wanderers or itinerants. Many of them became missionaries. One of the most notable was Columba (c. 521-597), who founded the monastery on the island of Iona (563), off the coast of Scotland. From here others went forth to evangelize and establish monasteries throughout the north of Britain. Lindisfarne, off the coast of Northumbria, was the most notable. Other traveling Irish monks brought the influence of Celtic monasticism to Gaul,

Germany, and Switzerland. One monk celebrated in legend, Brendan, may have come as far as America.

Benedict

The man who was to prove most influential in shaping western monasticism, St. Benedict, was born at Nursia in central Italy around the year 480. Benedict had studied in Rome as a young man, but abandoned student life for that of a hermit. He settled in a cave at Subiaco, learning about the ascetical life from a monk who lived in the neighborhood. As Benedict's reputation grew, others gathered around him, seeking his direction. Ultimately he organized them into twelve communities, each presided over by an abbot.

Because of a conflict with a local priest, Benedict moved from Subiaco to Monte Casino, a mountain overlooking the old road from Naples to Rome. Here he established the famous monastery, destroyed by the allied bombardment during the Second World War, where he wrote his Rule. His sister Scholastica, also an ascetic, established a monastery for women close by at Plombariola.

Benedict's Rule was not simply the product of his own experience. He was familiar with a number of contemporary rules and drew heavily on one composed early in the sixth century, known as the *Rule of the Master*. His own Rule, written in a terse Latin spiced with epigrams, is famous for its balance and moderation. Comprised of a prologue and seventy-three chapters, it describes a monastic life which integrated work and prayer, solitude and community, personal responsibility and authority.

A Benedictine monastery was essentially a self-contained community. The monks lived in a complex of buildings usually built around a open courtyard or "cloister."[14] The monks worked, studied, or walked in the covered passages which formed the sides of the cloister. The chapter house, refectory, kitchen, and a "warming room" were located on the first level; the monks's dormitory and "reredorter" or lavatory, usually built over a diverted stream, were located on the second story. The dormitory was connected to the church by a "night stairs," through which the monks could descend to the choir for the first office.

The monks elected one of their number to the lifetime office of abbot and lived under his direction. Communities of women lived under an abbess. The monastic day was divided into three parts. In the first place was the *opus Dei* (work of God), the monastic office. Eight times each day the community would gather in the church to chant the psalms in praise of God. Second, several hours each day were given to the *lectio divina* (divine reading), the spiritual reading which was to nourish a life of prayer. Benedict mentions the Bible, *the Lives of the Fathers,* Cassian, and the Rule of St. Basil. Finally, each day some seven hours (less in Winter) were devoted to manual labor.

The introduction to the Rule describes the monastic life as "a school for God's service." The topics treated in the subsequent chapters include the role of the Abbot, obedience, silence, humility, various offices in the monastery, and all the particulars of monastic life. The Rule provided for two meals a day in the summer, one in the winter months. The meals were eaten in silence, while one of the monks read to the community. After dinner a siesta was permitted. Each monk was to have suitable clothing, two tunics and cowls, of heavy material for the winter, lighter for the summer. They were to sleep in their habits, in a common dormitory lit by a burning candle. Prospective members, after a brief period in the community, were admitted to the novitiate for a year of testing and formation, after which they would pronounce their vows.

The Monastic Office

Twelve chapters in the Rule are devoted to the divine office or "choir," sung in the choir of the church. Prayer has always been at the very heart of the monastic life. From the earliest times, the monastic day was framed by prayer, based on the psalms, at dawn and again in the evening before retiring. Hermits prayed the psalms in the privacy of their cells, or with occasional visitors; communities would say or chant them together. Monks making vigils prayed the psalms in the silence of the long nights. From this tradition, probably rooted in the Jewish practice of praying at morning, noon, and night, the divine office was to develop.[15]

By the fourth century in the East, and soon after in the

West, daily offices were being celebrated in both the monasteries and in the major churches. The *Apostolic Constitutions* (380) from Syria near Antioch lists three cathedral offices; morning praise (matins or lauds), evening prayer (vespers) and a Sunday vigil of the Resurrection. The basic structure of an "hour" of the early cathedral office would have included several psalms and canticles, the Gloria in excelsis, some intercessions, closed by the blessing and dismissal.[16] Psalm 62 was generally prayed at morning prayer, Psalm 140 at vespers. The celebration of the cathedral office included chanting, incense, processions, and the symbolic use of light, particularly the lighting of the evening lamp. The early monastic office was less liturgical; it was generally longer and more contemplative.[17]

The structure of the office has remained basically the same since this early period, though it has been expanded by the addition of the minor hours, more psalms, antiphons, responsories, and scripture readings. In Benedict's time the monks rose for the first office, called vigils or nocturns at 2 a.m. (3 a.m. in summer), descending from the dormitory to their stalls in the candle-lit choir by way of the night-stairs. At dawn the monks returned to the church for lauds. The shorter hours of prime, terce, sext, and none broke the day, calling the monks from their work. At the end of the day came vespers, and just before retiring, the short office called compline. Benedict's rule said little about the Eucharist. It was celebrated only on Sundays and major feasts.

Benedictine Monasticism

Though the monastery at Monte Cassino was destroyed in 577, Benedict's Rule gradually spread as it was adopted by other communities. In 596 Pope Gregory the Great, himself a monk prior to his election to the chair of Peter, sent a group of monks to England under St. Augustine. They settled in southeastern England and founded a monastery and cathedral see at Canterbury. From here, after a number of setbacks, the church was reestablished in the south of England. In the north and center of England, Celtic missionaries from Lindisfarne were at work.

As England became more Christian, tensions began to develop between the older Celtic traditions of the north and the Roman and Benedictine traditions of the south. A conflict between the two traditions over the date of Easter led to a synod at Whitby in 664 which resolved the issue in favor of the Roman practice. From this time on, the Roman practice was to prevail. Those monasteries which had been founded in the Celtic tradition gradually adopted the Benedictine rule, without losing the missionary spirit which had come with the Irish monks. From England monks again went travelling, bringing the church and Benedictine monasticism to Germany, as monasteries were established at Echternach near Trier (698), at Fulda (744), at Hersfeld, and at Heidenheim in Württemberg. Benedictine monasteries began to appear throughout Germany and France.

In the eighth and ninth centuries many Benedictine monasteries became quite wealthy. They were now an established part of early medieval society and offered important social services. They provided hospitality for travelers and food, clothing, and shelter for the indigent. Because literacy was essential for the *opus Dei* and the *lectio divina* and with the accumulation of manuscripts copied and often illuminated by the monks, the monasteries became centers of learning and art. Wealthy or noble families often sent some of their children to live in monasteries as oblates; in the process many of them received an education in classical as well as Christian sources. Many of them remained as monks and nuns.

But with prosperity came also new problems. Not all those entering the monasteries came with the same religious motivation. The introduction of the private Mass, increasingly celebrated on a daily basis, led to a clericalization of the monastic life; those who had originally lived as lay monks were increasingly ordained as priests. The daily monastic office or choir began to demand more time as it became more elaborate. With less time available for manual labor, many monasteries became dependent on serfs and tenants for the cultivation of their fields and other menial tasks. Interference by wealthy benefactors frequently did considerable damage to monastic discipline; often they controlled monasteries they had endowed by appointing relatives as abbots. Many monasteries became powerful estates in the feudal economy.

Cluny

There were various efforts at reform, not always successful. In 814 Benedict of Aniane (750-821) was made abbot-general by Louis the Pious; three years later the Benedictine Rule was imposed on all the monasteries of the Carolingian empire. The most significant reform was that carried out by the monastery in Burgundy, not far from the modern city of Macon, known as Cluny. Founded in 910, Cluny was from the beginning placed under the jurisdiction of the pope and so was protected from both lay and episcopal interference. The reformed Benedictine life that developed there under a succession of very able abbots soon made Cluny a center of monastic renewal. Other independent Benedictine houses first consulted, then affiliated with Cluny, which meant acknowledging the authority of Cluny's abbot. What resulted was the first religious "order," a Cluniac order recognized by Pope Urban II in 1088. By the early twelfth century nearly fifteen hundred monasteries were affiliated with Cluny.

The Cluniac reform had established a network of thriving monasteries across Europe. Never had the monastic life assumed so important a position in the life of the church. No longer on the periphery, it was at the center. The Cluniac monasteries were prosperous; their elaborate choral offices celebrated in magnificent churches were understood as fulfilling an important social function, interceding for other Christians and making satisfaction for their sins. The great, third abbey church dedicated at Cluny in 1130 was one of the largest churches in Christendom. But the very success of Cluniac monasticism as well as the changing social conditions in the eleventh century as a feudal, village-centered economy began to give way before the new prosperity of the growing cities led a number of Christians to turn again to the roots, not just of the monastic movement, but of the church itself.

Some sought to return to the desert where monasticism had begun. Thus new communities of hermits began to appear. Others, like the Cistercians, attempted to live again the Rule of St. Benedict in its pristine simplicity. Some, in focusing on what was being called "the apostolic life" (*vita apostolica*) would develop new forms of monasticism, or more accurately, new Christian communities.

Monastic Reform Movements

The memory of the desert and the solitude it offered, as well as a dissatisfaction with contemporary monastic life, burdened by its inherited practices and compromised by its wealth, led a number of reformers in the tenth and eleventh centuries to establish new communities of hermits.

The New Hermits

In Italy, Romuald of Ravenna (c. 950-1027) began what was to become the first western eremitical order. Romuald had lived for a time in a Cluniac monastery, but left it unsatisfied. After reading the *Lives of the Fathers* he began living as a hermit, eventually settling at Camaldoli in the Tuscan hills. The monastery he founded there around the year 1010 was to be the motherhouse of a unique monastic community which combined the cenobitic and eremitic life. Some members lived together, following the Rule of St. Benedict. This core community provided the center and support for others who, faithful to the community's vocation to solitude and contemplation, lived some distance away as hermits. A hermit would live, work, and pray in his hut or garden, emerging only for occasional community functions. This has remained the basic pattern for the life of the Camaldolese hermits today.

Perhaps the most successful community of hermits was the Carthusians. Behind the Carthusians stands Bruno of Cologne (1032-1101) who left his position as chancellor of the cathedral school at Rheims about 1080 to join a group of hermits. In 1084 he and his companions sought solitude high in the Alps. Bruno was called to Rome by Pope Urban II but his hermits received fresh leadership when Guigo, dean of Grenoble, joined their community. Elected prior in 1109, he moved the community to its present location lower in the valley and built the monastery called La Grande Chartreuse after an avalanche in 1132 devastated their original settlement, killing some of the monks.

The Carthusians, as they were subsequently called, lived as hermits, each in his own cell. The monks assembled three times a day for the major hours of the office, praying the others privately in their cells. On feastdays they came together for Mass and meals. A Carthusian monastery is easily recognizable by its large cloister surrounded by the cottages or cells of the monks. Each cottage had a workroom, bedroom, latrine, and small garden.

Though never numerous because of the austerity of their life, Carthusian monasteries were established throughout Europe. Seven "charterhouses" were established in England during the fourteenth and fifteenth centuries. To this day the Carthusians claim to be an order never in need of reform because of their strict observance (*numquam reformata quia numquam deformata*). Their Rule, based on the Benedictine Rule modified in light of their own customs and others borrowed from the Cistercians, was compiled by Guigo and approved by Pope Innocent II in 1133. La Grande Chartreuse remained the motherhouse of the order. The monks were expelled from there for the last time in 1903 by the anti-clerical government of Clemenceau, returning in June 1940 just before the area was occupied by the German army.

Robert of Arbrissel (c. 1060-1117), another hermit turned itinerant preacher, anticipated the mendicant movement of the thirteenth century. He lived for a while as a hermit in Brittany and then began wandering through the Loire Valley barefoot, bearded, tattered and shaggy, preaching the apostolic life. Robert was not popular with the hierarchy because of his emphasis on penance and asceticism, but his message struck a chord with many men and women who joined him as members of "Christ's poor." They lived as hermits under his direction, among them, a considerable number of women.

Prior to this time there were few opportunities for women wishing to live what we now call the religious life. Most medieval monasteries were for men, and those founded for women were usually restricted to the wealthy and well-born.[18] Robert's preaching was welcomed by women from all walks of life, many of whom joined his movement. But his practice of allowing men and women to live in the same community soon occasioned opposition on the part of local bishops.[19]

To meet their objections Robert established a monastery at Fontevrault around 1100. Fontevrault was not the first monastery to include men and women in the same community; such "double" monasteries had existed in Egypt, at Kildare in Ireland, and had flourished in Gaul, Spain, and England in the early Middle Ages, only to disappear after the Viking invasions. Fontevrault represented a return to this tradition. The community was led by women abbesses; they exercised jurisdiction over both women and men. Some of the women were contemplatives, others penitents and reformed sinners. The men included priests and lay brothers who provided sacramental and material support for the community. Though Fontevrault did not last more than twenty years as a double monastery, the community continued to grow both in members, mostly aristocratic women, and in dependent houses.

The Cistercians

Not all reformers in this period saw the eremitical life as the only way to renew monasticism. There were many who saw monastic communities as called to a simple life of work and prayer and sought to return to the primitive spirit of the Rule of St. Benedict. The most successful effort was that begun by a group of dissatisfied monks, including their abbot, Robert, who left the monastery of Molesme in Burgundy in 1098 to found a new monastery at Citeaux (*Cistercium*). Known as the Cistercians, or "White Monks," to distinguish them from the Benedictines who wore black habits, they established an order which was to be the most influential in the monastic life of the twelfth century.

From the beginning Robert and his companions sought to develop a community different from the Cluniac community they had left. And in so doing they set what was to be the pattern for the Cistercian life. The site they chose was isolated, a undeveloped forest area. Their church was to be simple and austere, without the rich art, statuary, colored glass, and great towers of the Benedictines. Similarly, their liturgy was stripped to the basics. They shortened their choral office to allow more time for manual labor, dropping the needless repetitions and elaborate style that had developed especially under the influence of Cluny. Liturgical vessels were to be of silver rather than gold, crosses of wood, vestments of simple material. No one under sixteen years of age was to be accepted, thus no child oblates and no monastic school.

Though the first years at the "new monastery" at Citeaux were difficult, the community was blessed with a number of able leaders. After the monks at Molesme successfully petitioned the pope for the return of their former abbot Robert, he was succeeded first by Alberic (d. 1109), and then by Stephen Harding, an Englishman who became abbot in 1108. In 1112 the charismatic Bernard of Clairvaux arrived at Citeaux with thirty relatives and friends. In spite of his anti-intellectualism, Bernard was a gifted writer and preacher who drew the attention of many to the order. Under the capable administration of Stephen, the community began a rapid expansion. In 1113 a second community was established at La Ferte, and a year later another at Pontigny. In 1115 Bernard established a monastery at Clairvaux and became its abbot, a position he held until his death in 1153. By that time the order had 339 houses, 68 of which were abbeys dependent on Clairvaux.

One reason for the success of the Cistercian movement was that it attempted to recapture the essential simplicity of the monastic vocation. Cistercians felt themselves called to the traditional monastic life of work and prayer. They did not take on pastoral responsibilities. They sought solitude in the desolate regions to which they withdrew to build their monasteries.

Another reason can be found in the Cistercian understanding of community. In the writings of Cistercians like Bernard, William of St. Thierry, and Aelred of Rievaulx—to name just a few—there is a new emphasis on compassion, love, and companionship within the community as a help towards spiritual growth; in other words, there is a new stress on interpersonal relations.[20] Among the works of Aelred was a treatise on friendship.[21] Bernard is credited with bringing emotion and a focus on the humanity of Jesus into Christian spirituality;[22] he was also one of the first to address the virgin Mary as "Our Lady." The Cistercians developed a tender devotion to Mary. They have always dedicated their churches to her, and close their day by singing the *Salvae Regina* before her lighted image in the darkened church. This quiet moment at the end of Compline remains one of the most beautiful moments in the monastic day.

An important feature of Cistercian life was the large number of lay brothers, called "*conversi.*" Like other orders at this time, the Cistercians accepted uneducated men as brothers who took the habit and simple vows. The lay brothers were excused from singing the monastic office, followed a different schedule, and did much of the heavy work in the monastery and its fields. They had their own place in the church, separated from the monastic choir by a screen, and a part of the cloister was reserved for their use. Many such men who previously would have been excluded from the monastic life were drawn to the Cistercian houses where they were able to live as religious in a community which took responsibility for their material and spiritual needs.

The lay brothers often outnumbered the choir monks, as is evident from the size of the lay brothers' dormitory and refectory, separate from that of the choir monks, at sites such as Fountains in England and Maulbronn in Germany. It was largely through their labor and creativity that the originally barren locations of the Cisterican monasteries throughout Europe were drained, planted, and transformed into flourishing estates which had considerable impact on local economies.

The Cistercian reform also provided new opportunities for religious women. Monasteries of women following the Cistercian usages appeared early in the history of the order. There were some attempts in the thirteenth century to limit their number, but without much success. By the end of the Middle Ages, the number of convents almost equalled the number of monasteries. These convents, or others influenced by Cistercian spirituality and practice such as Helfta in Saxony, were to produce a number of mystics, among them Lutgarde of Aywires (d. 1246), Gertrude of Helfta (d. 1302) and Mechtild of Hackenborn (d. 1298). The spirituality of these women focused on the humanity of Jesus in a way that foreshadowed and influenced the development of the devotion to the Sacred Heart.

Cistercian government, expressed in Stephen Harding's "Charter of Charity" (1114), departed from the Cluniac model, with its abbot-general to which all the houses were subject. Cistercian abbots continued to be responsible for the daughter houses established by their communities so that power in the order was dispersed among the abbots of the more important houses. All the abbots were required to gather annually for a chapter at Citeaux. However the Cistercian nuns were excluded from the order's government; their communities were supervised by the male abbots.

The order by the time of Bernard's death had spread throughout Europe. By 1500 there were some 738 Cistercian monasteries and 654 convents.[23] But like the Cluniacs before them, the Cistercians became the victims of their own success. Discipline was frequently relaxed. The land they reclaimed and the gifts they received from their benefactors made them wealthy. Privileges exempting them from ordinary church government and from paying taxes on land given to the abbeys brought them enemies. Rather than poor monks, they became great landowners engaged in commerce, borrowing money, pursuing their claims in the courts of law, sometimes even evicting peasants living on newly acquired land.

The Cistercians represented the major force in the religious life of the twelfth century. But the social and cultural life of Europe was changing rapidly, and new communities were emerging, particularly the friars whose presence in the great universities of Europe was attracting many who might formerly have entered a monastery. The order remained strong, but history had passed the torch to the Franciscans, Dominicans, and other mendicant groups. Many of the great Cistercian abbeys did not survive the Reformation; others gradually lost members and were closed as Europe became more secular. The map of Europe is dotted with signs of the order's presence, beautiful cloisters and churches of silent stone at Senanque, Silvacane, and Le Thoronet in France, Fountains and Rievaulx in England, Maulbronn and Eberbach in Germany, Poblet in Spain (still open), all reminders of the glory of Citeaux.

But the original order has survived, and a reformed community of the strict observance known as the Trappists, because of the important role played in the seventeenth century by the Armand-Jean de Rance, Abbot of La Trappe in France, was eventually to bring new vitality to the Cistercian tradition.

Conclusion

The impressive story of all those drawn to the monastic life in the history of the church and the important role they played in the development of European civilization can easily blind us to what the monastic impulse is all about. In the simplest terms, it is the hunger of the human heart for the presence of God. Once this is experienced, all else becomes secondary. Being a monk has always had far more to do with a life of solitude, prayer, and evangelical simplicity than with cloisters, choirs, and cowls. And yet, from the earliest days of the church those who have been moved by this impulse have joined together in monastic communities to support and learn from each other.

The men and women who withdrew to the Egyptian and Syrian deserts in the third and fourth centuries, the noble women who gave themselves to prayer and ascetical discipline in Rome, the Celtic monks who created a monastic church in Ireland and parts of England, the Benedictines and later the Cistercians in their magnificent monasteries, the hermit monks at Camaldoli and La Grande Chartreuse, those in mixed communities of men and women like Fontevrault—these men and women, like people in every age of the church, were saints and sinners and often a little of both.

As monasticism and the religious orders which developed from it became an accepted part of both church and society, many came to the communities because of social exigencies not identical with a religious vocation. The monastery was a ideal place for a landless son or an unmarriageable daughter. But at its best it was also, as Benedict had taught, a school of the love of God. A life of work and prayer, modeled on the gospels, nourished by the liturgy, lived in community with others who came seeking the face of God often brought out the best in very ordinary men and women.

The very success of the monastic movement was repeatedly to prove its undoing. Self denial and personal poverty became meaningless against a corporate wealth which provided a life secure, comfortable, and lacking in challenge. But always new groups emerged, to start again, seeking through solitude and prayer the hidden God.

And it continues today.[24] To some, in a secular world the monastic life seems irrelevant, useless, a contradiction of all that is human. To others, sensitive to the impulse at its heart, contemporary monastic life seems not radical enough, too protected, institutionalized, and isolated from those very issues which a life lived in God's mysterious presence ought to address.

In his final years Thomas Merton struggled with these questions. He had entered a community whose way of life had changed little since the seventeenth century and saw perhaps more deeply than many of his contemporaries the implications of the Second Vatican Council for both the church and the religious life. The external changes—those which affected monastic silence, cloister, dress, discipline, the office—were less important. What really mattered was a recovery of the fundamental charism of the monastic life, a life of seeking God in solitude and deep prayer. The monastic vocation involves not a flight from the world but rather a critical distance from it; it should result in the inner freedom which opens a person to the social reality of the modern world in all its tragedy and threat, as well as its joys and hopes.[25]

At the end of the turbulent sixties Merton faced the social reality of his world "head on." His writings—which include over fifty books—touched on the inability of so many to believe, militarism, the threat of nuclear war, and the oppression of millions in the Third World. In the heady freedom of the years following the Council he fell in love with a young nurse and struggled to come to terms with his own affectivity.[26] He was involved with the peace movement during the war in Vietnam and attempted to develop a theology of non-violence. At the same time he was attracted by the wisdom of the East and was studying Buddhism. His death, twenty-seven years to the day he entered the Abbey of Gethsemani, came during a trip to the far East which was the final stage in a lifelong pilgrimage.

Thus Merton was very much a part of the twentieth century, but he faced it precisely as the monk he remained to the end of his life. Shortly before his death he wrote about the charism of the monastic vocation which his own life so well exemplified: "The desert of the monk is his monastery—and his own heart.

Yet in that desert he is free to encounter and love the whole world."[27] For many men and women today, the monastic life continues to be a living sign of God's abiding presence in the midst of the world.

Trappists in choir, Vina, California

3

Medieval Europe:
Evangelical Communities in the Cities
and Towns

In the twelfth and thirteenth centuries Europe underwent a transition which was to have a profound impact on the church. The cities of Europe began to come back to life. During the long centuries following the collapse of the Roman empire, with its commerce and its networks of communication, European life had been concentrated in small, rural communities. The feudal manor or estate, the country village, and also the monastery—each was a self-sufficient community with an established hierarchy and an assigned place for every member. But the focus of life began to shift back towards the cities as the eleventh century was drawing to a close. As people began moving to the cities to become traders, merchants, bankers, artists, craftsmen, clerks, bureaucrats, scholars and students, European life and culture began to take on an increasingly urban character.

A number of factors contributed to growing importance of the cities, the most important of which was the revival of commerce. The conversion to Christianity of the tribes and peoples who had been pillaging Europe in the North, West, and East freed much of Europe from the constant danger of barbarian raiders. Greater security made possible a revival of trade along the sea coasts and up the river valleys. New farming techniques which increased agricultural production also contributed to the growth of commerce. As money became the basis of exchange for goods and services, the practice of minting coins with a value determined by the issuing government became widespread. The cities, with their bankers, money lenders, and merchants, became important commercial centers. They also became centers of learning, as the new universities in cities like Salerno, Bologna, Paris, Oxford, and Cambridge took the place of the monastic schools.

But the revival of commerce introduced a number of new problems. The emergence of the profit motive was to challenge Christian morality and the understanding of Christian life itself; what was to be the Christian attitude towards wealth, personal property, and money lending?[1] The new prosperity had broken the stable pattern and strict hierarchy of European life and introduced several new social groups. The merchants, bankers, entrepreneurs, and professionals such as lawyers and civil servants constituted a middle class whose new status was based on their involvement in commerce and its necessary services.

At the same time an urban proletariat began to develop. Many peasants were drawn to the cities where they became engaged as artisans, traders, and laborers in the new industries. But not all were successful in making the adjustment to urban life, and without the relative security and network of family and social relations of the feudal manors, many became part of an underclass of unemployed or unskilled workers, vagabonds, and beggars. This marginalized group was to remain a volatile element of medieval society.

The new wealth and affluence affected the higher clergy just as much as it did the laity. Too many bishops and abbots flaunted their wealth and seemed more concerned with guarding the power of their offices than with carrying out their pastoral or religious obligations. As the gap between the wealthy and the poor continued to widen various voices, some prophetic, others demagogic, were raised in the effort to recall the church to an evangelical simplicity and apostolic poverty.

The Vita Apostolica

At the center of the unrest and ferment was a vision of the life of the primitive Christian community, usually referred to as the "apostolic life" (*vita apostolica*). But the vision was differently perceived.

The monastic tradition had identified the monastic life with the life of the apostles and the early church since at least the ninth century; both involved a common life, common prayer, and personal poverty.[2] Rupert of Deutz (d. 1129), called his treatise on monastic life *On the Truly Apostolic Life,* and other eleventh and twelfth century monastic theologians used this definition of the apostolic life to defend traditional monasticism in a rapidly changing world. For these theologians, the apostolic life or life of the gospels was primarily the *vita communis,* the common life, which provided for a corporate rather than personal ownership of property and possessions, as in the monasteries. There was little emphasis on the office or function of preaching.

But around the middle of the twelfth century others, both clerics and lay people, began to appropriate the vision of the apostolic life for themselves, though with an new emphasis on preaching, especially itinerant preaching, in imitation of the apostles. Europe began to experience an evangelical awakening.

A primary concern of this new understanding of the apostolic life was radical poverty, in imitation of the poor Christ. According to M.-D. Chenu, these new apostles addressed themselves to the new poor, the small merchants, landless nobles, and wage earners, those in the shops and hovels of the cities who were not merely economically poor but also marginalized because they had lost their fixed place in the old order.[3] For Leonardo Boff, those involved in these evangelical movements were moving beyond generosity towards the poor in the direction of actually taking their part; they were "the precursors and founders of the modern preferential option by the Church for the poor and oppressed."[4]

Thus there were many voices calling for a reform of the church on the basis of apostolic poverty in the twelfth and thirteen centuries. Too often the various movements have been lumped together as the many faces of medieval heresy, "Albigenses, Waldenses, Manicheans, Cathars, Paterini, Humiliati, Poor Men of Lyons, Bogomiles, Piphles, Jovians . . . ."[5] But the reality is more complex. Some efforts were successful, others were not. The reforming spirit carries its own dangers. But many of these movements were motivated by a genuine evangelical concerns.

Some were able to express their vision through traditional religious forms. Robert of Arbrissel, one of the first reformers, treated earlier in this text, gathered both clerics and lay people, men and women, reformed prostitutes and celibates into a group known as "Christ's poor." The monastery he established at Fontevrault in 1100 for his community became the first foundation of a new monastic order.

The new regular canons represented another reform based on a traditional model. They were secular priests, the clergy of the large urban churches and cathedrals, who adopted personal poverty and a communal, monastic life, based on the example and Rule of Augustine. Norbert of Xanten (c. 1080-1134), founder of the Premonstratensians or Norbertines, was typical; he seems to have wanted to combine Augustine's Rule with the *vita apostolica*. Norbert's canons were to engage in an active pastoral ministry, though their lifestyle was monastic. Though the order grew rapidly after Norbert's death, later Premonstratensians seemed to have placed less emphasis on preaching and pastoral work than on traditional monastic withdrawal. Dominic, the founder of the Dominicans, began as a cathedral canon.

Other reformers, carried away by the emotions their movements generated, ended up in irreconcilable conflicts with church authorities or by adopting teachings contrary to the church's faith. Arnold of Brescia (c. 1100-1155), a fiery preacher of apostolic poverty, tried to use political force to reform the church. He insisted that the clergy strip themselves of political and economic power and live on alms alone, going so far as to argue that no monk or cleric who owned property could be saved. In his efforts to limit ecclesiastical authority he became involved in two revolutionary communes, first in his native Brescia in 1138 where he led a revolt against the bishop and later in Rome where he became the leader of a commune called the Roman Republic which drove Pope Eugenius III from the city. Arnold was executed in 1155 by Frederick Barbarossa.

Likewise the Catharist movement seems to have been marked from the beginning by the strong current of dualist teaching which their more orthodox contemporaries saw as Manichean. They rejected material possessions, the eating of meat, and sexual relations as well as the hierarchical authority, teaching, and sacraments of the church. Yet as Lester Little points out, they considered themselves Christians and their desire to live a simple life, besides being shared with many others in their time who were drawn by the ideal of the apostolic life, may have been inherited from the monastic tradition which taught the same kind of personal renunciation.[6]

If the twelfth century was a time of false prophets, heretical teachers, and revolutionary millenarians who rejected the church, or ended up outside it, it was also a time of a genuine evangelical revival. In a sense, many Christians were rediscovering the radical Gospel and were attempting to live it out in the new situation of life in the city. But if what was emerging was an urban spirituality, it was also a spirituality which had a decidedly lay character.[7] These were lay men, not interested in the clerical state or the now clericalized monastic life, and women looking for an alternative to the usual choice of either marriage or a convent. Both were drawn by the vision of the *vita apostolica.* For many of them, preaching belonged to the very nature of the apostolic life. As they attempted to live it out, they established new communities. Some were lay, while others eventually became recognized canonically, which made them "religious." We will consider some of these communities and their founders.

Evangelical Communities

Humiliati

About the year 1170 a movement of people known as the "Humble Ones" or Humiliati appeared in Milan and soon spread throughout the cities of Northern Italy. Not unlike the contemporary charismatic renewal, the Humiliati included both lay people and clerics in a conscious effort to live a life patterned on the Gospel. Many of the lay members were from the upper classes. Some were married and continued to live with their families; single members lived together in communities. Many of them were drawn to the movement from the Italian cloth industry and continued to work in it to support themselves. They also devoted considerable time to the service of the disadvantaged. Their manner of life was simple; they wore undyed clothes, refrained from political life and litigations, and recited the canonical hours.

Yet in one respect the Humiliati were unusual; they encouraged preaching, by their lay members as well as by those who were ordained. This intrusion on what was understood as the office of the clergy provoked a strong reaction. In 1179 Pope Alexander III forbade them to preach in public. His successor, Lucius III, included them and the Waldensians in a 1184 condemnation of a number of sects which refused to acknowledge any right of the hierarchy to regulate preaching.

But in 1201 Innocent III, sensitive to the various groups of "poor men" seeking to live the apostolic life, gave the Humiliati the status of a religious order. He divided them into three separate grades, one of clerics, another of celibate lay people, and a third of married people who lived with their families. He also approved of their practice of lay preaching on the basis of a distinction he drew between preaching in the area of doctrine (*articuli fidei*) and exhorting others to a life of piety and good work (*verbum exhortationis*).[8] By the end of the thirteenth century there were communities of Humiliati in most of the Italian cities engaged in the cloth industry, particularly in the North.

Waldensians

A similar movement originated in Lyons, France. Its founder, Peter Waldes, was a wealthy merchant and land owner, one of the richest men in Lyons. After a conversion experience which is thought to have taken place during a severe famine which hit Lyons in either 1173 or 1176, Waldes gave up his business, compensated those he had taken advantage of, and began distributing food to the hungry in the streets of the city.

Naturally Waldes' action occasioned considerable comment among his fellow businessmen, and he was quick to take advantage of their discomfort. He began preaching, though it is interesting to note that he had to hire a priest to translate the gospels for him so that he could learn them by heart. He was soon joined by others from all walks of life who were attracted by his new evangelical lifestyle. They imitated his example and began preaching themselves—men and women, the learned and the uneducated—and soon, these "Poor Men of Lyons" were preaching everywhere.

The issue of lay preaching was to lead ultimately to their separation from the church. Already disillusioned by the wealth and lack of zeal of so many of the clergy, the Waldensians represented an evangelical lay fraternity. From their point of view, preaching was an intrinsic dimension of the apostolic life they sought to lead. On the other hand, church officials considered preaching the proper office of the clergy and saw these new itinerant preachers, most without education or theological training, as a potential source of heresy, as well as a threat to the church's hierarchical structure. Waldes and his followers won approval from a synod convened at Lyons in 1181 but after a disagreement with the new archbishop of Lyons they were excommunicated and denounced to the pope. In 1184 they were condemned along with the Humiliati at the Council of Verona.

Nevertheless the movement continued to spread; there is evidence of Waldensian activity in north-eastern Spain and northern Italy as well as in southern France. Waldensians in Italy later joined with some of the unreconciled Humiliati and were known as the Poor Lombards or Italian Brethren. Unlike the French Waldensians from whom they separated in 1205, the Poor Lombards were able to own their homes and property. They also continued to support themselves through manual labor, forming workers cooperatives. From Italy some Waldensians established communities in southern Germany. Waldensian communities still exist in Italy today; they consider themselves precursors of the Reformation.

Some of the Waldensians were later reconciled with the Roman church. After a debate between Waldensians and Catholics near Toulouse in 1207 in which Dominic was involved, Durand of Huesca, an apologist for the Waldensians, formed a group of evangelical preachers called the Poor Catholics. They were approved by Innocent III in 1210 and allowed to preach, though under episcopal supervision. A group of Poor Lombards led by Bernard Prim was reconciled in the same year.

Though the early Waldensians were fierce in criticizing the affluence of the clergy, doctrinally they had not departed significantly from the tradition. Nevertheless, their style of life and emphasis on lay preaching challenged the clerical state and even called it into question. Later some seemed to have argued that evangelical laymen could preach, bless and consecrate without ordination.[9] The tragedy is that the official church was not able to recognize what this and other evangelical movements were trying to say. When Waldes appealed to the pope in 1179 for approval of his movement, Walter Map, a British cleric involved in the Roman hearing, described his followers in words which some thirty years later could have been used of the first Franciscans: "These people have no settled abodes; they go about two and two, barefoot, clad in woolen, owning nothing, but having all things in common, like the apostles, nakedly following a naked Christ."[10]

Beguines

A tourist today wandering through Ghent, Louvain, or Bruges in Belgium would find it hard to miss the large settlement at the center of each city known as the *beguinage*. The center of Amsterdam has its *beginjnhof*. A beguinage is well described as "a town on a miniature scale, with the church as the hub."[11]

Many of them were begun outside the walls of the city. Small houses built side by side formed the perimeter; inside were streets lined with houses, a square, cemetery, and the buildings needed to support a community life such as a church, hospital, workshops, and convents for the poorer members of the community. In the thirteenth century there were beguinages throughout Belgium and Holland as well as smaller communities or houses in the cities of the Rhineland and northern France.

Who were the Beguines? Caroline Walker Bynum refers to them as the first women's movement which can be identified in Christian history.[12] Though they have been described as "semi-religious,"[13] they were actually lay women who, influenced by the *vita apostolica,* lived together in community, practiced celibacy and a mild form of voluntary poverty, and sought to live an evangelical life. The movement seems to have had its origin in the desire of women in the cities of the Low Countries to form pious associations. Whether living with their parents or in small groups, they attended Mass and the office in the parish church and gave themselves to a simple way of life and charitable works. At the end of the twelfth century many of them began to live together in communities.

Originally many of those who became Beguines came from the upper classes; they were daughters of the new middle class families. As the movement spread and became more organized, beguinages appeared in many of the cities and towns of the Low Countries and northern Germany. Towards the end of the thirteenth century an increasing number of poor women were accepted into the Beguine communities.

The movement cannot claim a single founder. The holy woman Mary of Oignies (d. 1213), who lived as a lay sister in a house of canons in the diocese of Liége, was very influential in the development of the Beguines. She influenced James of Vitry who seems to have won initial approval for the Beguine way of life from Rome in 1216. Formal approval came from Pope Gregory IX in 1233. Yet there were those, particularly among the more conservative members of the clergy, who did not welcome the idea of religious women not living in traditional convents, doing apostolic work. They were frequently criticized and even accused of heresy.

Despite occasional tendencies towards a standardized monastic way of life, the Beguines did not have a rule. Some houses had episcopally approved statutes, but their lifestyle remained informal. Unlike women living the monastic life, they did not take public vows. Many authors stress that their observance of chastity was part of their evangelical lifestyle, but they were free to leave and marry if they so chose. Their poverty was not severe. A woman of means who wished to become a Beguine generally was expected to provide for the construction of a house where she lived simply but comfortably. The house became part of the community's property upon her death. Some members worked outside the community, usually in the textile industry, to provide material support. They promised obedience to the rules of the house or to the head mistress and were subject to their local pastor in religious matters. They were expected to remain in the community they chose to enter.

Their religious practices included daily Mass and the canonical hours, though like most people in the Middle Ages they received communion less frequently. They wore a habit which consisted of a simple dress of a plain, beige color. Yet they had considerably more freedom than religious women in monastic communities and convents as they were not confined by rule to the cloister. They also engaged in various ministries to the sick and the poor.

While it is true that the movement provided an alternative lifestyle for many women not interested in marriage or a traditional convent as well as a home for sick and destitute women, it should also be said that many women were drawn to the beguinages because they shared the desire of many of their contemporaries to live an evangelical life that was nourished by Scripture and lay in its orientation.

The Beghards constituted a similar movement, though much less organized. In Germany especially the Beghards included both men and women, laboring people of diverse backgrounds, many of them itinerants. They were not as popular or as widespread as the Beguines. The Council of Vienne in 1311 condemned certain teachings of both groups, though the Beguines later won a qualified approval.

The Brethen of the Common Life, a movement in many ways similar to the Beguines, flourished in the Netherlands and Germany in the fourteenth to sixteenth centuries. The Brethren lived in mixed communities of priests and laymen. Though they did not take vows and their communities were not canonically recognized by the church, they sought to live a Gospel life. They ministered to others through preaching and a literary apostolate, the copying of manuscripts which also provided support for their communities. They were influential in the development of the *Devotio Moderna*.

The New Orders

Franciscans

Like Peter Waldes in France, Peter Bernardone was a wealthy merchant in Italy who had made a considerable amount of money in the cloth trade. Bernardone was content with his life as a businessman. But he was having trouble with his son, Francis. An extremely promising if boisterous youth, Francis had been brought up to carry on the family business in Assisi.[14] But in his early twenties he underwent a complete transformation. A recurring illness and a number of dreams left him a changed man. To his father's frustration, he began to spend considerable time in solitude, devoting himself to prayer, and giving whatever he happened to have in his pockets to the poor.

Matters came to a head after Francis sold a horseload of his father's expensive cloth-and the horse as well-in neighboring Foligno and tried to give the money to the priest at San Damiano, a church where he used to go to pray. Francis went into seclusion, but after a month his father found him, demanded that he return the money, and turned him over to the local magistrates to have him punished. The magistrates referred the case to the local bishop. When Francis and his father appeared before the bishop in the square of Assisi, the bishop, after listening to Bernardone's complaints about his son, advised Francis to give up all his property. Francis immediately went into the bishop's palace, took off all his clothes, and returned stark naked to stand before his father, the bishop, and all those present. Laying his clothes and some money in a bundle at the feet of the bishop, Francis stated that henceforward he would serve only God.

From this point Francis, his nakedness covered by a cloak given him by the bishop, became the Poverello, the little poor man. But it took some time before the precise kind of life to which he felt himself called became clear to him. His restlessness in the following months betrays his own searching. He lived for a while at a monastery where he served in the refectory. Then he moved to a house for lepers where he ministered to its inhabitants. Later he returned to San Damiano and stayed there, dressed as a hermit and calling others to join him in the task of rebuilding its damaged church, refusing the meals the poor priest there offered him and begging to support himself.

In 1208, having finished at San Damiano, he moved to another church. This one, known as Santa Maria degli Angeli or the Portiuncula, the little portion, was an abandoned ruin. Francis set about restoring it. At this point he seems to have been more interested in the hermit's life than in the *vita apostolica*. But on February 24, 1209, the Feast of St. Matthias, a visiting priest was celebrating Mass at the Portiuncula and read from Matthew 10:7-9:

> "As you go, make this proclamation: 'The kingdom of heaven is at hand.' Cure the sick, raise the dead, cleanse lepers, drive out demons. Without cost you have received; without cost you are to give. Do not take gold or silver or copper for your belts; no sack for the journey, or a second tunic, or sandals, or walking stick. The laborer deserves his keep."

The next day Francis began to preach in Assisi. Before long he had a group of companions wandering the Umbrian countryside with him, preaching in the town squares, working in the fields with the peasants and begging for what they could not earn by their labor, and coming together frequently at the Portiuncula. To give some direction to their way of life Francis drew up what has been called the primitive rule; it was based on three texts from the gospels (Matt 19:21; Lk 9:2-3; and Matt 16:24) and some simple directions on the vows and the common life. In 1210 he brought his little group of "lesser brothers" (*fratres minores*) before Pope Innocent III in Rome and received his approval for their way of life. From this humble beginning was to develop the Franciscan order.

In 1217 the movement began sending friars to various countries. As they spread through Europe they divided the community into different provinces, each governed by a minister or superior. A chapter held in 1221 brought together some 3,000 friars. But there were already internal tensions in the movement which would later split it. Many of those attracted to the movement were moved by the same spirit which drew others to the Humiliati, the Poor Men of Lyons, and other evangelical movements. With only a brief rule, no formal probationary period or novitiate, and minimal structure, it was difficult to assure that new members would be formed in the ideals shared by Francis and the first companions. Radical poverty, itinerant preaching, and mendicancy offered an evangelical freedom, but this very freedom was also open to various abuses.

Other early Franciscans, among them an increasing number of educated brothers, urged greater structure and some kind of religious regularity or conventual life to form new members in the spirit of their founder. They urged Francis to write another, more detailed rule. In 1221 he produced what has become known as the First Rule, really an expansion of the primitive rule. As in the earlier rule, the brothers were forbidden to own houses, exercise authority, or receive money in any form. The new rule required a year of novitiate formation and prohibited wandering about without permission. Each member received two habits (one without a hood), a cord, and trousers. They were to be of poor quality. Those who were educated were required to recite the office; the others repeated the Our Father and some other prayers. Preaching was to be regulated by the minister and the laws of the church.

Still some of the brothers found the rule of 1221 not sufficiently precise and lacking the careful canonical language necessary to win the approval of the Roman Curia. So Francis went to work again, this time assisted by Brother Bonizo who was a trained canonist. This "Second Rule" or "*Regula Bullata*," approved by Pope Innocent III in 1223, became the official rule and gave the Franciscans the status of a religious order. Earlier, wandering Franciscans had been mistaken at times for members of other suspect evangelical fraternities, particularly the condemned Waldensians, while their lack of education left some to unknowingly identify themselves with heretical movements.[15] Francis' rule served to preserve the Franciscan movement and integrate it into the church.

But Francis' charism was difficult to institutionalize. How poverty was to be observed continued to be a source of division and led later to interminable debates over whether or not Jesus and the apostles had actually owned the goods they used. Related to this was the question of what was necessary for the apostolic life. As early as 1230 the order had to petition Rome for a mitigation of the poverty demanded by the rule. This relaxation was the first of many, the inevitable consequence of the struggle between the absolute poverty of the rule and the responsibilities of administering a widespread order, maintaining churches, educating its members, caring for its sick. Another problem was the tension between the original lay orientation of the movement and the increasing number of clerics. Finally some were drawn more towards prayer and contemplation while others sought to adapt the order to the exigencies of its pastoral ministries.

Within the order various factions emerged. A strict observance group, called the Zealots, was later known as the Spirituals. On the other extreme was a group favoring mitigations of the rule, represented by the famous administrator Brother Elias who built the basilica at Assisi which would have embarrassed Francis. Finally there was a more moderate group generally referred to as the Community. The radical Spirituals, with their demand for absolute poverty and their high regard for the unstructured community of the early days, in many ways resembled the evangelical fraternities, particularly the Waldensians. Frequently controversial, some of their members became involved with heretical movements. They disappeared after 1325.

The struggle to institutalize the Franciscan charism continued over the centuries. The group known as the Community gradually resolved itself into the Conventuals who permitted the communal owning of property, including the "convents" in which they lived, and the Observants. The latter gained a quasi autonomy in 1446 and became independent in 1517 as the Friars Minor of the Observance. The Capuchins began as a reform in Italy in 1525; they gained canonical status in 1528 and became independent in 1619. Other Observant reform communities, among them the Discalced, Recollects, and Reformed, were finally united in 1897 as the Order of Friars Minor.

Francis appeared at a providential moment in the life of the church of the thirteenth century. A number of authors have pointed out that the reception Francis received at Rome from Innocent III was quite different from that Peter Waldo received thirty years earlier from Alexander III, even though both men and their followers shared a similar vision.[16] It is important not to overlook the urban roots and social implications of the spirituality of Francis.[17] He and his followers sought to identify with the poor to whom they ministered; their monastery was the world, and particularly the urban world with all its unique problems.

But Francis was also a man of immense personal and religious appeal. His spirituality was simple and evangelical, characterized by a gentleness and compassion which expressed itself in his love for the poor and made him speak even to the animals of the forest as his brothers and sisters. He understood from his own prayer the value of affectivity, image, and symbol; he gave us not only the beautiful Canticle of Brother Sun but also the Christmas creche. In many ways Francis combined the values of the *vita apostolica* with contemplative focus on the person of Jesus crucified; he was able to so completely embody the Gospel in his own life that in his final days the marks of Christ's passion appeared in his own body. His movement did much to renew the church in the thirteenth century.

Dominicans

If the Franciscans were characterized by a devotion to poverty which included an identification with the poor, the Dominicans were identified from the beginning with preaching and education. A contemporary of Francis, Dominic de Guzman was born at Calaruega about 1170 of a noble Castilian family. He was educated in Spain and became a priest and cathedral canon of the diocese of Osma. What was to become the Dominican order grew out of his own involvement in the struggle against the Albigensians in France, and with what Dominic consequently came to see as the need of the church.

At that time much of the south of France was in turmoil. Both the Waldensians and the clearly heretical Albigensians were actively engaged in missionary activity. The name Albigensian was given to a Catharist movement centered in the city of Albi. The Albigensians had begun a parallel church with their own bishops and deacons and their own rites, including an initiation ceremony known as the *Consolamentum*. Like Catharists elsewhere, they preached a dualist theology which held that the spiritual soul was imprisoned in a material body from which it had to be freed. They rejected material possessions, marriage, and the eating of meat and eggs. Their leaders, known as the "Perfect," lived in great austerity, modeled on the poverty of the apostles. Of course their manner of life contrasted considerably with the wealth and pomp of many higher clerics.

Dominic's first contact with these movements came in 1203 while passing through Toulouse on a mission to Denmark with his bishop, Diego of Osma. His innkeeper turned out to be an Albigensian and Dominic spent most of the night bringing him back to the faith. On their return from a second mission to Denmark in 1206, after a stop in Rome, Dominic and Diego met three papal legates at Montpellier, all Cistercians, sent by Innocent III to counter the growing Albigensian movement. The Cistercians were discouraged; they related to the two travelers how their opponents would constantly frustrate their preaching by bringing up examples of the scandalous behavior of the clergy. Bishop Diego responded by suggesting that their own lifestyle might have something to do with their lack of success. He urged them to rid themselves of their horses and retainers and offered to join them himself,, promptly dismissing all members of his party but Dominic.

Diego convinced the Cistercian legates, and they went forth to preach two by two, Diego and Dominic, and two of the Cistercians. The third had to return to Citeaux. In debates held at Montreal and Pamiers in 1207 they had some success; at Pamiers two influential Waldensians returned to the church, Arnold of Crampagna and Durandus of Huesca. Diego died after a year but Dominic continued his itinerant missionary work through the cities of southern France.

The Dominican order grew out of the group of missionaries who joined Dominic. They lived an itinerant apostolic life, owning only what they could carry with them, and begging to support themselves. Dominic went barefoot until the Council of Montpellier ordered that shoes be worn, to distinguish orthodox preachers from the heretics who identified the right to preach with going barefoot.[18] He apparently inherited the leadership of a community of women converted from the Albigensians which Diego had established at Prouille in the diocese of Toulouse. This community, like similar communities run by Albigenisan women, served as a place of rest for the missionaries. Thus in many ways the early Dominicans resembled the Albigenisan and Waldensian missionaries they were preaching against.

In 1215 Dominic first sought papal approval for his community. Simon Tugwell relates a story of the confusion of Pope Innocent III when Dominic asked that he recognize his community as an Order of Preachers (*Ordo Praedicatorum*). Since bishops were still generally assumed to be the only official preachers, the pope wondered to himself why this man wanted to found an order consisting entirely of bishops.[19] Though Rome was following a policy of not approving new religious rules at the time, Dominic's community, having adopted a modified version of the rule of Augustine, was approved by Pope Honorius III in 1216.

The next year Dominic sent the friars to preach throughout Europe. His singling out the cities of Paris and Bologna, both distinguished by their universities, was to give a distinctive character to his order. The friars came to the university of Paris to study, but before long some of their members were joining the faculty as masters. By 1230 Dominicans held two chairs of theology there. Other masters and students, drawn to hear the Dominican preachers at their collegiate church of St. Jacques, joined the order in large numbers and deepened its commitment to the intellectual life. Before long Dominican theologians like Albert the Great and Thomas Aquinas were drawing students from throughout Europe. The order played a major role in developing the theology of the schools or "scholastic theology" which was to provide a needed alternative to the prevailing monastic theology.

The Dominican way of life, partly monastic, partly accommodated to the demands of the apostolic life, was particularly conducive to a life of teaching and scholarship. Canonically they were "clerks regular," that is, an order of religious priests engaged in active ministry, though they also had religious brothers. Over the canon's white habit Dominicans wore a white scapular and cowl and a black cowled mantle, open in front. They followed the Rule of Augustine, like other canons of their time, but complemented it with a carefully developed structure of customs and statues which became their Constitutions. Dominicans promised stability to the order itself, not to a particular house as monks did.

Dominic modeled his Customary on that of the Premon-stratensians which he had followed earlier, though he modified it considerably. He omitted the sections on manual labor and on government. His friars were to sing the office in choir, but "briskly and succinctly lest the friars lose devotion and study be in the least impeded."[20] To encourage study, priors were allowed to dispense friars from the rules for fasting and diet, even if necessary from choir and the office. Special rules were added for both teachers and students. Each priory was required to have a professor in residence.

The first general chapter at Bologna in 1220 made poverty absolute; Dominicans were not to own property or have fixed revenues. Their government was remarkably democratic. They organized themselves into provinces and elected their superiors at the level of priory, provincial chapter, and general chapter. Though the provinces were relatively autonomous, a master general assisted by a curia served as a major superior for the order. Other communities including the Franciscans came to imitate their governmental structures. Raymond of Penafort gave juridical form to the first constitutions in 1241.

Dominic died in 1221 but his order continued to grow rapidly. By 1228 there were Dominican provinces of Provence, France, Spain, Lombardy, Rome, England, Germany, Hungry, Poland, Scandinavia, Greece, and the Holy Land. By 1347, the beginning of the Black Death which was to devastate both the Dominicans and the Franciscans, the number of the former was above 21,000.

Second and Third Orders

Franciscan and Dominican Women

By introducing a new kind of active religious order, both Dominic and Francis freed at least male religious from the confines of the monastic cloister. They were not as successful in making it possible for the many women drawn to their orders to live fully the apostolic life.

One of Francis' closest friends was Clare, a young woman from the noble Offreduccio family of Assisi. In 1212, at the age of 18, Clare made her own renunciation and joined Francis.

Other women followed; they worked with the brothers of Francis in attending to the needs of the poor, though they lived in their own community at San Damiano. The "privilege of poverty," given them by Innocent III, really meant that they could exist as a community without the usual corporate holding of possessions. Such corporate ownership provided a basis of support, but it also meant being subjected to the traditional rules and regulations governing religious life. The privilege of poverty gave them a certain freedom from this ecclesiastical regulation.[21]

But within a few years the active ministry of the Franciscan women was curtailed. In 1219 the cardinal protector of the Franciscans, Cardinal Hugolino, gave them a rule, Benedictine in orientation, which required them to accept property, and thus convents to live in, and imposed the obligation of cloister. Though the "Poor Clares" were to flourish as a cloistered contemplative community, this enforced monasticization was unfortunately to befall many other communities of religious women dedicated to works of mercy. Only in the nineteenth century were active congregations of religious "sisters," as opposed to contemplative "nuns" able to gain official ecclesiastical recognition as religious. Clare herself fought for the remainder of her life to have her own rule accepted, with its provision of absolute poverty. Innocent IV approved it in 1253, two days before her death.

Women's communities in the Dominican tradition were monastic from the beginning. The first community at Prouille, founded by Dominic's bishop, Diego, was for women converted from the Albigensians. Though they supported the missionary preachers working with Diego and Dominic, the community was strictly enclosed. Dominic established monasteries for nuns at Rome, Madrid, and probably at Toulouse. These communities were understood as supporting the apostolic work of the friars through their prayers. Unlike the community at Prouille they did not serve as way stations for the missionaries; the order now had lay brothers to maintain houses for the preachers.

After Dominic's death in 1221 the number of monasteries or convents of women in the Dominican tradition continued to grow. New communities were established. And at a time when the Cistercians were becoming increasingly unwilling to undertake the direction of religious women, many existing communities, particularly in Germany, affiliated with the order. Some had been communities of Beguines. Not all of them shared the same Dominican vision. They seem to have been more often communities of women who looked to the friars for direction and instruction rather than communities formed and animated by the same charism. These enclosed communities were brought together under one constitution by the Dominican Master General Humbert in 1257 and became the Dominican Second Order.

Tertiaries

The Dominican Third Order, like its Franciscan counterpart, developed out of the penitential movement which Francis did so much to popularize. Many lay men and women, moved by Francis' preaching, sought to lead simple lives of prayer and service themselves, based on the Gospel. This led to the formation of associations of lay men and women who sought to live an intense spiritual life "in the world." The Beguines and the Beghards belonged to this same lay movement. These fraternities and sororities devoted themselves to caring for the poor and sick; their hospices provided basic social services for the poor of the medieval cities.

The penitents welcomed the new friars, both Franciscan and Dominican, who often assisted them in their work on behalf of the poor. The penitents provided direct service and financial support while the friars offered spiritual guidance to the penitents and pastoral care for the poor they served. The status of the penitents was recognized as early as 1221. They were to recite the office, hear Mass monthly in their associations, and receive spiritual direction from the religious. They were also granted certain privileges, among them, an exemption from military service. Though not technically religious, many of them wore a religious habit and observed celibacy.

The mendicants, particularly the Franciscans, were initially reluctant to take on the responsibility for the penitential associations. They did not want to loose the freedom to pursue their own apostolic goals and feared incurring financial obligations.

They also did not want to become entangled in the considerable controversies which arose between the different associations over finances. But a rule for Franciscan tertiaries was approved in 1289. The Dominicans also took on officially the direction of those penitents attracted to their spirituality and provided them with a rule in 1286. These "Brothers and Sisters of Penance of Saint Dominic" then became part of the Dominican family, a third order with their own formation programs, vows, religious obligations, and Dominican directors. In 1434 they became Third Order of Penance of Saint Dominic.[22]

Conclusion

The evangelical awakening that swept through Europe in the twelfth and thirteenth centuries was both enormously fruitful and at the same time divisive. It was significant in a number of ways. First of all, the *vita apostolica* called men and women not just to the witness of an evangelical poverty in their own lives, but in many cases to a solidarity with the economically disadvantaged. Francis of Assisi remains to this day a symbol of this evangelical poverty in the life of the church.

Secondly, there was a decidedly lay character to this evangelical movement. Many of the communities to which it gave rise were lay communities. Some, such as the Humiliati, the Waldensians, and the Poor Catholics, were mixed communities. Others, communities of lay women like the Beguines, can be seen as representing for the first time a genuine movement of women within the church. The efforts of these communities to develop and live an evangelical lay spirituality were to give rise to a number of tensions between themselves and the official church.

Lay preaching became an issue, and for a while was provided for, thanks to Innocent III. At the same time the abuses that sometimes accompanied the itinerant, often uneducated lay preachers led to specific prohibitions and a closer linking of preaching to the office of the ordained.

Both Francis and Dominic were moved by the new evangelical spirit which influenced so many of their contemporaries.

The notion of an apostolic community free to go where there was need, preaching the Gospel in the towns and cities, living in poverty and simplicity like the apostles did not originate with either of them. But they were particularly successful in finding ways to incorporate this vision of the apostolic life into the structural life of the church.

Dominic's community was primarily clerical from the beginning. But the "lesser brothers" of Francis underwent a clericalization necessitated in large part by the requirements of their preaching mission. This contributed to a controversy over the original spirit of the founder which was to introduce lasting divisions into the community. The life of the "lesser sisters" was changed even more radically. Though Clare ultimately won for her sisters the privilege of poverty, it is clear that the church was not yet ready to recognize a group of religious women living an apostolic life similar to the Franciscan brothers. The Poor Clares were required to accept cloister.

Though the new mendicant orders did much to revitalize religious life in the thirteenth century, their subsequent histories show the same pattern we saw earlier in the case of the monastic communities; an initial fervor which attracted many and led to rapid growth. But with success and numbers came also material prosperity and too often a loss of zeal. Discipline was relaxed and too many accommodations were made. By the sixteenth century religious life had deteriorated markedly.

4

The Reformation

By the sixteenth century the need for a reformation of the religious orders was evident to many. Far too many of the monastic communities had become comfortable homes for the unmarried sons or daughters of the wealthy; many had lost any semblance of religious discipline, regular prayer, or community life. The mendicants, particularly the Franciscans and Dominicans, fought with each other over theology and the question of which community practiced most perfectly the poverty of the Gospel. Meanwhile the figure of the ubiquitous fat friar had become a popular joke.

But when the Reformation came, coincidentally out of a Augustinian monastery in the person of a German monk Martin Luther, it rejected the religious life in general and monasticism in particular. Though his thinking developed gradually, Luther formulated his objections to monasticism in a treatise published in 1552 called *De votis monasticis judicium*[1] First, he argued that monastic vows suggested a superior way of life, different from that of ordinary Christians, and so was contrary to the word of God. Second, he saw the monastic life itself as an effort to justify oneself before God, and hence, contrary to his doctrine of justification by faith alone. Third, he felt that the vows were contrary to Christian liberty. His treatise was to have an enormous influence, particularly on religious.

John Calvin's views on monasticism were similar to Luther's. In Book IV of the final version of his *Institutes,* published in 1559, he presented a systematic rejection of monastic vows.

Since monastic vows were in his view unlawful and super-
stitious, they could not bind.[2] In some of his other works,
Calvin in the often intemperate language of the sixteenth
century, subjected monks to considerable ridicule; he accused
them of laziness, lechery, of having bloated faces and bellies,
of being consumed with concupiscence. Calvin objected particularly to the vow of celibacy which represented for him a
rejection of the divinely instituted state of marriage. He also
felt celibacy was a violation of Christian liberty, for it committed young men and women to a way of life which many of
them would not be able to faithfully live out.[3]

Much of the Reformers' rejection of monasticism was
focused on the vow of chastity. Luther seems to have begun
with a protest against mandatory celibacy for pastors and
moved to a rejection of all ecclesiastical celibacy and monasticism itself. Calvin stressed the many failures in the observance
of the vow and the tensions involved in trying to live a celibate
life. All of them stressed Christian freedom. One hears similar
arguments today. But what one misses in them is any sense
that a life of celibacy for the sake of the kingdom might be
worthwhile. The Strassbourg reformer Bucer seems to have
recognized the possibility that a person might be called to a life
of continence, but Biot points out that he made the decision to
remain celibate so much dependent on the individual that any
obligation to abide by that decision was excluded. His position
also seemed to exclude any religious community which had
real authority over its members.[4]

On a deeper level, the Reformers used the doctrine of justification by faith alone to argue against the monastic life in
principle, and with it, the spirituality which monasticism
implied. Their objections to monasticism became permanently
enshrined in the confessional documents of their churches.
The usually irenic Augsburg Confession (1530) concludes a
long, polemical discussion of monastic vows as follows:

> Thus there are many godless opinions and errors associated
> with monastic vows: that they justify and render men
> righteous before God, that they constitute Christian perfec-
> tion, that they are the means of fulfilling both evangelical
> counsels and precepts, and that they furnish the works of

supererogation which we are not obligated to render to God. Inasmuch as all these things are false, useless, and invented, monastic vows are null and void.[5]

The confessional statements of the Reformed churches are less explicit, but similar sentiments can be found.[6]

The Reformation in England did not seek to exclude monasticism on theological grounds. Henry VIII simply suppressed the monasteries. In 1536 there were over eight hundred monasteries and religious houses in England and Wales, housing some ten thousand monks, canons, friars, and nuns. By April of 1540 there were none. The suppression was carried out legally through a number of acts of parliament. Though it began under the guise of a reform, in fact it amounted to an enforced nationalization of the religious houses. The monastic buildings and properties were taken over by the crown and sold, to pay off royal war debts. The new owners frequently stripped the lead from the roofs of the monastic buildings, melting it down with fires fed by the roof timbers. Without roofs to protect them from the elements and used as stone quarries by local residents, the monastic buildings soon fell into ruin. Their remains dot the landscape of England to this day.

Thus within a relatively few years religious community life practically disappeared in those parts of Europe embraced by the Reformation. Monastic property was conficscated and secularized. In England most of the monks and nuns were turned out of their houses and given small pensions; only a few resisted, or tried to carry on their religious lives. In Europe thousands of monks and nuns left their monasteries and convents, many to enter into marriage as did Luther himself. Even when those belonging to the new communities established in the sixteenth century are included, the number of religious men decreased from roughly 250,000 to 200,000 in the hundred years between 1475 and 1575.[7] Many communities disappeared entirely.

Some few communities survived within the Reformation. The community of the Augustinian monastery of Möllenbeck, near Rinteln, embraced the Reform in 1558 and continued to live the monastic life, virtually unchanged for another hundred years. The last monk of Möllenbeck died in 1675.[8]

But from the Reformation new forms of Christian community life were also to emerge. We will consider briefly two of them, those communities belonging to the radical reformation, and those communities issuing from and after the Catholic Counter Reformation, especially the Jesuits.

Communities of the Radical Reformation

From the "left wing" of the Reformation emerged another movement far more radical in its critique of traditional Christianity than that of Luther in Germany, Zwingli and Calvin in Switzerland and France, and the Anglican reformation in England. Generally termed the "Radical Reformation," this movement includes the Anabaptists, the spiritualists, and the evangelical rationalists.[9]

The Anabaptist movement originated in Switzerland, the result of a dispute in Zurich between Zwingli and other, more radical reformers. Also known as the Swiss Brethren, like other radicals they rejected infant baptism on the basis of their interpretation of Scripture; hence the name "Anabaptists." Far more important to them was the baptism of the Spirit, an inner experience of grace which was to precede adult baptism with water.

From Zurich the movement spread to other parts of Switzerland, to southern Germany and Strassburg, and to Moravia. The Anabaptists rejected the state-churches favored by the Calvinists and sought to live in free communities or "conventicles." They insisted on adult baptism and their right to be non-conformists. Because they refused to swear oaths and to do military service they were frequently persecuted for what was seen as their threat to public order. Among the various Anabaptists groups were the Moravian Brethren, the Hutterites, and the Mennonites.

The Spiritualists are most often associated with the name of Thomas Müntzer. Spiritualists emphasized the interior experience of salvation. Some of them so interiorized Christian life that they rejected all rituals, including baptism and the Lord's

Supper, thus anticipating the Quakers. Similarly, the Evangelical Rationalists stressed an extremely personal Christianity, individually disciplined and externally free. Some of them insisted on baptism by immersion.

Common to all of them was the conviction that the church had "fallen" with Constantine; what they sought was the restoration of the apostolic church of the New Testament. Often directed by lay leaders, they emphasized the priesthood of all believers and went a long way towards recognizing the equality of men and women within the community of faith. Their anticlericalism was directed not just against the priests and bishops of the Catholic Church, but against the other reformers as well. Their emphasis on the interior experience of the Spirit reportedly led Luther to exclaim that these "Schwärmer" or enthusiasts "had swallowed the Holy Spirit, feathers and all."

But they were quite serious about wanting to live the Gospel concretely in their every day lives.[10] The concept of discipleship, focused on the passion of Jesus, was primary for them. They saw their communities as alternative societies. Many of them were pacifists, refusing to bear arms. Their movement was marked by an egalitarian spirit and a strong concern for the poor, many of whom found refuge among them. Some of them, like the Hutterites, taught and practiced a holding of goods in common, like the primitive Christians of Jerusalem.

Their unconventional, often charismatic worship, the strong ethical dimension to their spirituality and the fact that they were often persecuted for their radical views gave them a unique sense of community that was over against the world and the other churches. According to Timothy George, for many of them "the Christian life was a kind of uncloistered monasticism that presupposed a daily walk of holy obedience, prayer, and praise."[11] Most of their congregations did not last beyond the sixteenth century, but their concern for Christian community within the world survives among Quakers, the Moravian Brethren, Mennonites, and others who are inheritors of their tradition.

Post Reformation Catholic Communities

The Reformation dealt the religious orders a serious blow.

Though many communities disappeared from history, most of the communities we considered earlier survived and new communities, different in their spiritualities and missions, appeared to call men and women to lives of discipleship, prayer, and service.

In Spain Teresa of Avila, a practical woman as well as a mystic later recognized as a doctor of the church, carried out a reform of the Carmelites. She was assisted by John of the Cross. Their reform was to reaffirm the value of the contemplative life in the church. A new reform of the Franciscans in 1526 produced the Capuchins.

A number of similar clerical communities were founded in the sixteenth century, among them the Theatines (1524), the Somaschi (1528), the Barnabites (1533), the Jesuits (1540), the Clerks Regular of the Mother of God (1583), the Camillians (1591), and the Piarists (1597). All told, some seventeen communities of men were established in the sixteenth century. They were to be active communities, rather than monastic or conventual communities. The most successful of these new communities of men was the Society of Jesus or Jesuits.

The Jesuits

A year before Columbus "discovered" America Inigo de Loyola was born to a family of minor nobility in the Basque region of Spain. His autobiography begins with the statement: "Until the age of twenty-six he was a man given over to vanities of the world; with a great and vain desire to win fame he delighted especially in the exercise of arms."[12] He began his first career when, as a teenager, he entered into the service of the royal treasurer of Spain as a courtier. Then, with his imagination filled with thoughts of glory, he took up the path of the noble man at arms.

In 1521, Ignatius was seriously wounded while defending the citadel of Pamplona against the French; a canon ball shattered one leg and damaged the other. During the long period of his convalescence at Loyola, during which he endured several crude surgical operations, Ignatius read several books that were to change his life. One was Ludolph of Saxony's *Life of Christ,* the other, Jacobo de Voragine's *Golden Legend,* a popular collection of the lives of the saints. Again his imagination was inflamed, but this time with a great desire to distinguish himself for Christ the King rather than for some worldly ruler.

He left Loyola in 1522, going first to Montserrat. In the great abbey church there Ignatius spent a night in vigil before the statue of Our Lady, at the end of which he gave up his sword. Dressed as a pilgrim he moved a few miles away to Manresa, a small town where he spent over a year, begging his food, helping the sick, and giving himself to long hours of prayer. Moments of great consolation alternated with periods of great dryness and desolation. As Ignatius gradually learned the ways of discernment in prayer, the ideas which would become the basis of his famous *Spiritual Exercises* began to take shape in his mind. Really a series of meditations on the gospels and exercises, designed to bring one into a new relationship of union with God, the book of the *Spiritual Exercises* was first published in 1548.

After a trip to the Holy Land and some encounters with the Inquisition, Ignatius began a long course of studies to prepare himself for a preaching ministry and the priesthood. His studies would give him first hand experience with some of the great universities of Europe. Beginning first with grammar at Barcelona, he continued his studies at Alcala, Salamanca, and finally at Paris (1528-35). What would ultimately become a new kind of religious order, the Society of Jesus, really began as a movement of university students at Paris. As Ignatius worked his way through the courses first in philosophy, then in theology, he began leading some of his fellow students through his little book of the *Spiritual Exercises.*

Among these students were Pierre Favre and the brilliant but worldly Francis Xavier. Xavier initially resisted Ignatius, with his persistent question, "Francis, what does it profit a man if he gain the whole world but loses his immortal soul?" But Francis eventually made the Exercises and they became friends and companions.

A long period of prayer together led seven of them to the resolution to remain together after their studies. They hoped initially to work among the Moslems in the Holy Land and promised to take three vows, poverty, chastity, and a promise to go to Jerusalem. If they could not go to the Holy Land, they resolved to place themselves at the service of the pope. On August 15, 1534 they walked to the little chapel in honor of St. Denis on Montmartre in Paris and pronounced their vows at the communion of the Mass celebrated by Pierre Favre.

Having obtained their degrees as masters of theology, they traveled to Venice. On June 24, 1537 they were ordained. While they waited for a ship they ministered to the sick in the hospitals and did pastoral work. When it became evident that a war between Venice and the Turks made their journey impossible, they went to Rome. They had already decided that their group would be known as the *Compania de Jesus,* the Company or Society of Jesus. As they continued their pastoral work and care for the disadvantaged in Rome, the success they enjoyed began to threaten the unity of their group. Various prelates sought their service.

In 1539, after another long period of prayer, referred to in Jesuit literature as the "Deliberation of the First Fathers,"[13] they decided to add a vow of obedience to one of their number, thus becoming in effect a religious order.

But their idea of a religious order was radically different from previous ones. Unlike other orders, the Society was not to have a distinctive habit, prescribed fasts and penances, or the obligation of choir. Jesuit religious life was based, not on a rule, but on the experience of the *Spiritual Exercises.* From the *Exercises* came a spirituality which taught them to seek and find God in all things. Mobility was to be key; they were to be ready to go wherever there was need, whether among believers or unbelievers. Already present was the idea that some would make a vow of special obedience to the pope for the sake of whatever mission he might give.

Ignatius drew up a "Formula of the Institute," outlining the religious life they proposed. The omission of choir troubled some of those appointed to examine the Institute as Ignatius presented it. For them it was inconceivable that a religious order would not gather in church regularly to pray the hours of the office. But the work the companions were doing drew praise from others. In 1540 Pope Paul III officially approved the Society in the bull *Regimini militantis ecclesiae.* A year later Ignatius was elected superior general.

In the years that followed, while Ignatius stayed in Rome, directing the community and working on what would be the Jesuit *Constitutions*,[14] the companions traveled on various missions throughout Europe and to India and Asia. In 1540 Ignatius told Francis Xavier that he was to go to the Indies, thus beginning the foreign missionary work which was to become so characteristic of the order. In that same year Pierre Favre went to Germany, initiating a Jesuit mission there which was to restore Catholicism to much of that land. In 1541 Alonso Salmeron and Paschase Broet undertook a difficult mission to Ireland.

The Jesuits, as they were soon known, were in demand, not only as reformed priests but also as professors and theologians. Claude Jay declined the chair of theology vacated by the death of Johann Eck at the university of Ingolstadt, but gave a series of lectures there which convinced him of the need for educational work, particularly in Germany. Diego Laynez and Alonso Salmeron served as official theologians to the first session of the Council of Trent which opened in 1545. From ten members in 1540, the Society grew rapidly. When Ignatius died in 1556 there were almost a thousand Jesuits in the community. Their mission was already worldwide; in 1556 Jesuits were working in India, Japan, Brazil, and Africa.

The long commitment of the Society of Jesus to education developed very early out of the colleges or residences established by Ignatius for the order's "scholastics," its young Jesuits in training. There was a Jesuit college at the University of Paris already in 1540, at Coimbra, Padua, and Louvain in 1542, in India, 1543, and at Cologne and Valencia by 1544.

At first these colleges were simply residences for the scholastics studying at the great universities of Europe. However very early lectures and classes were begun in these colleges because of the unhappy state of university education in the sixteenth century, with poor lectures, unorganized curricula, and inadequate direction of students. So successful were these Jesuit colleges that soon other students, lay and clerical, sought admission. They were admitted, as early as 1543 in India and 1546 at Gandia, Spain.

The number of these colleges had increased to forty-six by the time of Ignatius' death. This was just the beginning of the

Jesuits' commitment to education which was to win them the reputation of "the schoolmasters of Europe." Today the Jesuits run twenty-eight colleges and universities and some forty-two high schools in the United States and over 1,000 educational institutions worldwide. They are the church's largest order of men.

Apostolic Communities of Women

In succeeding centuries other communities of men and women were to imitate the commitment of the clerks regular to apostolic work. In the seventeenth century Vincent de Paul founded the Vincentians (1663) and with Louise de Marillac the Daughters of Charity (1643) to work with the poor and the sick. John Baptist de la Salle founded the Christian Brothers (1681) to educate the sons of the working classes. In the eighteenth century Paul Danei founded the Passionists (1725) and Alphonsus Liguori the Redemptorists (1735). In the nineteenth century some sixty-five clerical congregations and societies of priests were founded.[15]

Like Clare of Assisi in the thirteenth century, many religious women who wanted to devote themselves to charitable works encountered difficulties with the official church. In the seventeenth century it was unthinkable that religious women would venture beyond the confines of their enclosure or cloister. Distinctive religious habits, cloister, and choral offices were appropriate for contemplative communities, but those communities of women seeking to carry out active ministries in the cities and among the poor found these monastic practices contrary to their particular vocations. Yet frequently they had cloister and other monastic practices imposed upon them.[16]

Angela Merici founded the Ursulines in 1535 as an uncloistered community of apostolic women who took a vow of chastity, were dedicated to teaching, but lived at home with their families. A primitive rule was approved by Paul III in 1544. In 1572 Charles Borromeo requested that the Ursulines in Milan live in community; he gave them a rule which added cloister and a contemplative dimension to their teaching vocation. In France other independent Ursuline communities adopted this rule, becoming monastic in the process. By the beginning of the eighteenth century there were some 9,000 Ursulines in France living a life which was now strictly cloistered.

The story of the Visitation community, founded by Francis de Sales and Jane Frances de Chantal in 1610, is similar. The first women of the community lived together at Annecy but would leave their convent to care for the poor and the sick in their homes. When a second house was established in Lyons five years later, the archbishop required them to become a strictly enclosed order with solemn vows. Thus the women of the Visitation also became cloistered nuns.

The Daughters of Charity, the young women Vincent de Paul gathered to live a religious life with Louise de Marillac and minister to the sick in 1643, were to be lay women. Breaking considerably with tradition, de Paul wrote that they were to have "for a monastery the house of the sick, for a chapel the parish church, for a cloister the streets of the city or the wards of the hospital, for a grate the fear of God, and for a veil holy modesty." Though they lived a religious life in community, they dressed simply, in the costume of the peasant women of the Isle de France. It was only later that they were recognized as religious in the canonical sense.

The nineteenth century witnessed a tremendous revival of religious life, particularly in France. Though the old orders had been devastated by the revolution, more than 400 active congregations of religious women were founded in France in the period between 1800 and 1880.[17] But it was only after 1841, when the Sisters of Mercy received papal recognition, that congregations of sisters could be officially approved as religious.

Conclusion

Even though the Reformation represented a rejection of traditional religious life, the Radical Reformation produced its own alternative Christian communities. The Quakers, Moravian Brethren, and Mennonites today are descendants of these Radical Reformation communities.

The Jesuit order was the most visible Catholic religious

community to emerge during the period of the Catholic Counter Reformation. As active religious rather than contemplatives, the Jesuits adapted considerably the traditional forms of religious life.

Because their manner of life was taken from that of secular priests, they were known canonically as "clerks regular" rather than canons or friars. They abandoned the common recitation of the office and distinctive religious habits. They stressed mobility and obedience. But as mentioned earlier, they were not the only community of priests to move in this direction.

The period between Trent and the First Vatican Council saw the establishment of a great many communities of religious women dedicated to apostolic works. The official church did not always know how to respond to these women; often communities founded for the care of the poor and the sick or for the education of women were required to accept cloister and other monastic practices.

From the nineteenth century until the great changes in religious life which followed the Second Vatican Council, religious sisters provided a whole infrastructure of social and educational services for Catholics throughout the world. As Christian communities of dedicated women, they did missionary work, ran and staffed hospitals, schools and colleges, cared for the sick, the orphaned, the elderly, and the disadvantaged. Their contribution to the life of the church has been enormous.

5

Protestant Monastic Communities

If it is true that new religious communities have appeared at moments of ferment or crisis in the church's long history, then the twentieth century has been no exception. This century which has seen two world wars waged between nations at least nominally Christian, a holocaust which almost exterminated the Jewish people, the blinding light and apocalyptic power of the atomic bomb, used against two Japanese cities in 1945, as well as the pervasive materialism and secularism in many western democracies has hardly been an age of faith.

Religious practice has suffered considerably. In some European countries where church practice was once expected, the reverse is now true; to be a practicing Christian is to take a countercultural position. When Pope John Paul II visited France for the first time as pope, he asked rhetorically, "France, eldest daughter of the church, are you faithful to the promises of your baptism?" Only 15 per cent of French Catholics practice their faith. In Italy roughly 15 per cent of those between the ages of 15 and 30 attend Mass regularly. And in England, on the basis of the percentage of church goers to general population, there are more people worshipping on any given Sunday in the Soviet Union than in the Anglican Church.

Christian Communities in the Twentieth Century

But the twentieth century has also seen a number of signs of the enduring dynamism of the Gospel, working like a leaven kneaded into the dough. From a meeting of Protestant Christians concerned with missionary work in Edinburgh in 1910 was to grow the search for Christian unity known as the ecumenical movement. It led to the foundation of the Faith and Order Movement at Lausanne, Switzerland in 1927 and to the establishment of the World Council of Churches at Amsterdam in 1948. The most dramatic religious event of the century was the Second Vatican Council (1962-65), called by Pope John XXIII to renew the Roman Catholic Church and to commit it to the search for Christian unity. And the century has seen the appearance of a host of new Christian communities.

In part the appearance of these communities can be related sociologically to a greater movement towards community which reflects the isolation and alienation experienced today by so many people. The causes underlying this phenomenon are deeply rooted in western culture. They include the breakup of the traditional family, the isolation of modern life, whether in the suburbs or in the cities, the pervasive secularism of our culture, and the inability of people to enter into lasting relationships. The communes of the late 60s and the cults and new religious movements of the 70s and 80s are also part of this phenomenon.[1] It is clear that not every community movement religious in nature has been a healthy expression of the Christian life.

But the sociological reasons are not sufficient to explain the phenomenon. The communities we are concerned with here represent new and different instances of that same impulse to live out the Gospel in a radical way that we have seen earlier in this book. They are quite diverse in their forms and orientations and therefore not always easy to classify. Some are new expressions of the traditional monastic life. Some have been formed out of a desire to support a life of ministry to the poor and marginated or have gathered those working for social justice. Some are communities of the poor themselves, finding in the Gospel both hope and empowerment, becoming in the process a new way of being "church."

Some are "religious" communities in the traditional sense of being communities of celibate men or women, living a life of prayer and worship, or sharing a common ministry. Others are "lay" communities, with the same diversity of purpose or function one finds in religious communities.

Covenant communities, coming out of the Charismatic Renewal, resemble some religious communities in that they exist to enable their members to live the Gospel more intensely; their unity comes from their life, not from their mission. Others are service or justice communities, gathered by a common ministry. But all have been nurtured by the Gospel and by the various springs and currents of renewal which have appeared in the twentieth century. We will consider first, some communities which would be traditionally called religious. Later we will look at a number of new lay communities.

Protestant and Anglican Communities

The Reformers' rejection of monasticism in the sixteenth century had been almost complete. A few communities such as the Cistercian community of Möllenbeck (1558-1675) near Rinteln in Germany realigned themselves with the Reform. Others were founded in the Reformation tradition. The Moravian community of Herrenhut was established on the estate of the Reformer Zinzendorf in 1722. Though the members did not hold their goods in common, they joined together for prayer, the study of scripture, and meals.

The first community of Protestant religious women, called "Deaconesses," was founded in Germany at Kaiserwerth in 1836. Celibacy was understood as being part of their vocation. This was also true of a group of French Protestant women, called the "Lazarists," founded by Antoine Vermeil (1842). These women lived a community life, committed themselves to obedience as well as celibacy, and held their goods in common. W. Loyd Allen speaks of these groups as constituting a "fragile bridge" over the chasm between the religious orders and the Protestant tradition.[2]

Thus the tradition of religious community life did not disappear entirely within Protestantism. Little known and not always successful, it remained an aberrant phenomenon. But in the twentieth century the combination of a number of renewal movements and several unique individuals was to lead to a Protestant recovery of religious life and monasticism.[3]

Like Luther, Calvin had sought to reform the liturgy. He called for vernacular celebration, introduced popular hymns, and stressed the importance of preaching. But with rare exception, the subsequent history of the liturgy in the Reformed tradition was more one of decline than of development.[4] Preaching came to so predominate that in the minds of many, even today Protestant worship is synonymous with a long sermon and a number of hymns. The secularism of the Enlightenment and the moralism of the nineteenth century both tended to further diminish the place of the Eucharist. If the Eucharist was celebrated at all, it was often an abbreviated rite tacked on to the "worship" service, almost as an afterthought.

The notion of spirituality was also viewed with suspicion. For many Protestants, the very concept of spirituality suggested a return to the old works-righteousness theology against which the Reformers had raised their cry in the sixteenth century. Though this is changing today, it is interesting to note that the only entry under "spirituality" in the *Book of Concord,* the official collection of the Lutheran confessional writings, is a negative one, referring to "false" spiritualities.[5]

Lutheran Pietism in the seventeenth century, largely a reaction to the arid scholasticism of Protestant orthodoxy, was one move in the direction of a more explicit devotional life. Pietism at least could be understood as planting the seeds of a new interest in spirituality. But the Reformation traditions generally continued to question the concept of spirituality and to resist any attempt to introduce liturgical prayer, the office, retreats, and other practices deemed monastic or "high church."

The result was that the Protestant churches did not generally have the resources of liturgical prayer and spirituality which could provide the communal focus and sustain those who might be drawn to some form of religious community. Simply put, a praying community needs a structure of common prayer to express its praise and worship of God. And it needs a practical vision of the Christian life or spirituality to sustain and nourish its identity. The liturgy, particularly the Eucharist, has provided a center around which Catholic communities could focus their communal lives. Anglicans have preserved the tradition of liturgical prayer by providing for the celebration of Morning Prayer and Evensong.

The Oxford Movement in nineteenth century England represented a conscious effort to realign the Anglican Church with its catholic heritage. With it came a restoration of religious life within the Anglican Communion. A community of religious women was formed in London in 1845. In the hundred years since a considerable number of religious communities have been established in the Anglican Communion, including more than sixty communities of Anglican sisters.

The Society of St. John the Evangelist (1865), more popularly known as the Cowley Fathers, was the first successful religious community of men. Some communities, such as the Order of the Holy Cross in the U.S. (1881) and the Order of St. Paul in England (1889) are monastic. Some, like the Community of the Resurrection (1892) are missionary congregations. Some are engaged in parish ministry. Some are Anglican versions of the traditional orders; among them are the Benedictines of Nashdom Abbey (1914), the Order of St. Francis (1919, U.S.A), the Society of St. Francis (1921), and the Anglican Poor Clares (1922, U.S.A.). There are Anglican congregations of sisters following the rule of St. Vincent de Paul and others the rule of Francis de Sales.[6]

Monasticism Rediscovered

Within the Reformed churches of France and Switzerland, a number of renewal movements in the period after the First World War were to lead to a new appreciation of liturgical prayer and spirituality as well as to a recovery of monasticism within the Reformed tradition.

One was the movement for a third order for Protestants begun by a French Reformed pastor, Wilfred Monod (1867-1943). Appealing to the examples of both Francis of Assisi and the Waldensians in the thirteenth century, Monod set forth his views in a pamphlet published in 1925.[7] Known as the "Veilleurs" or Watchers, his third order was to be a group of lay people with a rule—controversial for many Protestants—a spirituality based on the beatitudes, and a book of daily prayers. Though they were not to live in community, the Watchers would met regularly for prayer and sometimes for retreats. The movement caught on and spread through the Reformed churches of France and francophone Switzerland.

Another renewal movement, *Eglise et Liturgie,* was liturgical. It was begun in 1930 by a group of Swiss pastors and lay people from the canton of Vaud, three years after the first meeting of the Faith and Order movement at Lausanne. Two members of the group were to distinguish themselves as liturgical scholars. Jean-Jacques von Allmen was on the theological faculty of the canton of Neuchatel and helped spread the influence of the movement beyond Vaud. The other, Richard Paquier, became its spiritual guide. In 1931 the group began publishing a series of booklets of liturgical texts for the Sundays of the year as well as for the Baptism, Confirmation, and Communion services which were to have a considerable impact on the liturgies of Vaud, Geneva, Bernois Jura, and France.

The group also began developing a form of the divine office with services for morning, noon, and evening prayer, first published in 1942. Its principle author was Paquier. In 1953 a revised version was published as the common office of *Eglise et Liturgie* and the communities of Grandchamp and Taizé.[8] Though not all the Reformed congregations of Switzerland and France reflect the liturgical renewal begun by *Eglise et Liturgie,* the group has had a considerable impact on the liturgical commissions of the various Reformed churches. Perhaps more importantly, it has brought a new appreciation of liturgical prayer to individual Reformed congregations.[9]

A third movement, closely related to the other two, is specifically monastic. From a group of women who began meeting at Grandchamp, Switzerland, in 1936 a community of religious sisters was to develop. After the war, a community of monastic brothers was established at Taizé in France. Two of its founding members, Roger Schutz and Max Thurian, had been involved in *Eglise et Liturgie* as theological students. Both communities originated in the Swiss Reformed tradition.

Grandchamp

Just short of where the Areuse river empties into Lake Neuchatel, on the plain between the lake and the foothills of the Jura mountains in Switzerland, lies the little village of Grandchamp. The village consists of a number of Swiss multi-family farm houses and a large, barn-like structure, originally a drying shed for a local cloth-dying industry, arranged around a court with a fountain at its center. This is the home of a community of Protestant sisters known simply as the sisters of Grandchamp.

In 1931 a number of women interested in a more intense spiritual life, some of them members of the Veilleurs, came together in a house at Grandchamp for a retreat. At this time in the Reformed church, retreats were almost unheard of, but a pastor in Geneva encouraged one of the women, later known as Sister Marguerite, to open a house for those who desired to make retreats. In 1936 Sister Marguerite opened the house in Grandchamp, assisted by Sister Marthe. The two welcomed and assisted other women who would come to spend time in prayer and silence. Sister Irène joined them in 1940 and a small community began to take shape.

In 1944 Madame Léopold Micheli who had helped organize the first retreat at Grandchamp in 1931 joined the community. Later to be known as Mother Geneviève, her leadership skills and vision would make her the real founder of the Grandchamp community.

As these women at Grandchamp continued a simple life of prayer and hospitality towards those who came for retreats, other women were moved to join them. As their life together developed, it gradually took the form of a religious community. In 1952 eight sisters made their profession and Mother Geneviève was installed as the responsible sister or superior. A year later the community adopted the newly written rule of Taizé. Later they adopted a simple religious habit; light blue in color with kerchief and leather belt, it is similar to that to other European sisters.

A candidate lives with the community for a while before beginning the novitiate. The novitiate is of indeterminate length; profession is made when the novice is ready to make the commitment. Today the community numbers about sixty women from Switzerland, Germany, Holland, and France.

The heart of Grandchamp is its chapel, called "l'Arche" or the Ark. On the second floor of the large drying shed one enters a huge dark space with red, green, amber, and purple light streaming through the narrow colored glass panels opened into the chapel's walls. The sisters gather here four times a day for prayer, in the morning, at mid-day, in the evening before dinner, and for compline, using the office of Taizé. Kneeling on prayer benches or using the surrounding pews, they form a wide circle around the low altar. As at Taizé, they celebrate the prayer around the cross on Friday evenings as part of the "little Easter" which marks the end of each week.

The Eucharist is celebrated regularly. Behind the altar is the Rublev icon of the Holy Trinity and on the opposite wall a large bare cross and the Vladimir Madonna. The icons are lit by oil lamps.

Monastic Life

The life of the sisters of Grandchamp represents an open monasticism. They live in community, though families not connected with the community still live as neighbors in some of the buildings. They commit themselves to celibacy, to a sharing of all goods, and to accepting decisions made by the sister responsible for the community. The sisters also commit themselves to participating in the struggle for justice and human dignity, in so far as their contemplative life permits.

Their life is one of prayer, built around the four daily offices, and a ministry of hospitality to the guests who come to make retreats or simply to spend some quiet time in prayer. Some come for extended periods to share in the life of the community. The guests join the sisters for prayer in the chapel and take meals with them in their refectory, a simple room with wood tables, filled with sunlight. The welcome is always genuine and warm.

Because the sisters see themselves as particularly committed to reconciliation and Christian unity, there is a strong ecumenical dimension to their vocation. One of their particular gifts is their ability to appreciate and value different traditions of worship and spirituality. The sisters themselves come from the mainline Protestant traditions, Reformed, Lutheran, Methodist, and United Church.

In their early days they learned much from several Anglican

communities. Many of them took von Allmen's courses in liturgy in Neuchatel. Several of the sisters studied with the Orthodox theologian Paul Evdovkimov. From Orthodoxy came their appreciation of icons, their monastic theology, and much of their spirituality. Their office, lectionary, and emphasis on the Eucharist reflect the Catholic tradition. From the Protestant tradition comes a strong sense for the centrality of the word.

The spirituality of the sisters stresses not so much what they can achieve on their own, but rather what the Spirit works in them. But this calls for a disciplined struggle and an openness to continual conversion. In their contemplative focus on the person of Christ, the Orthodox concept of *theosis* or deification and the Gospel image of the Transfiguration are both important. They see their own transformation as a community in Christ as a sign and spiritual source for the transformation of the world.

The sisters have close relations with a number of Catholic communities. Mother Geneviève and some others spent time with the Little Sisters of Jesus in Algeria in the 1950s. Today the responsible sister joins in the annual meetings of the *Service des Contemplatives,* a meeting of the abbesses of Catholic contemplative communities in French-speaking Switzerland.

Not all the sisters live at Grandchamp. In 1954 a retreat house, called the Sonnenhof, was established at Gelterkinden, near Basel in German-speaking Switzerland. Others live in "fraternities" of two or three sisters, doing simple work and living a vocation of presence and prayer in various locations. In Switzerland they work at a psychiatric clinic, in Algeria they live with the poor, and in Israel they try to be a presence for reconciliation between Christians, Jews and Moslems. Other fraternities are in Lebanon, Holland, and Paris. Each August the sisters return to Grandchamp for a reunion.

Conclusion

Grandchamp is not the only monastic community in the Protestant tradition. The Marienschwestern of Darmstadt in Germany, known officially as the ecumenical sisterhood of

Mary, represents another example. Founded towards the end of the Second World War, these sisters live in community, give an hour each day to contemplative prayer, and come together several times a day for prayer in common. Throughout the day a prayer vigil is maintained by two sisters in a special chapel in their house. Their activities include catechatical work among the children of the poor, a publications ministry, and penance for the victims of war.[10] Other communities include Pomeyrol which also follows the rule of Taizé and Imshausen, a community which grew out of the German resistance movement.

Taizé itself is in a different category. Though it began as a monastic community in the Protestant tradition, it has become over the years a profoundly ecumenical community, with Protestant, Anglican, and Catholic members. We will consider Taizé in the following chapter.

The unwillingness of the members of Grandchamp to define themselves too narrowly has brought them at times considerable pain. But that price they have been willing to pay in living out their dedication to prayer and reconciliation.

In many ways Grandchamp and the other Protestant monastic communities have reappropriated elements of the tradition of the church catholic which had been lost to the churches of the Reformation. They have not always been understood by their churches. At times they have experienced resistance because of their emphasis on liturgical prayer, celibacy, and life according to a rule; too often these practices are seen as "Catholic" rather than simply rooted in the Gospel and the tradition of the universal church.

Still, their Reformation heritage continues to inform their life and spirituality. Though they have rediscovered the monastic tradition, they have always felt themselves free to develop their own forms and change them when necessary. They continue to stress personal values over institutional ones. A visitor experiences a certain freshness and spontaneity in their communities. The welcome is always warm, for like reconciliation, hospitality is an important part of their spirituality.

Cistercian Abbeys

1. Sénanque Abbey, 12th Century Cistercian, Provence

2. Silvacane Abbey, 12th Century Cistercian, Provence

Silvacane

3. Silvacane, Cloister
4. Church
5. Cloister gallery
6. Cloister arcade (restored)

Le Thoronet

7

8

9

7. Le Thoronet, cloister and lavatorium (washroom)

8. Fountain in lavatorium

9. Cloister gallery

Taizé

10. Taizé, Church of Reconciliation

11. Interior, Church of Reconciliation

Taizé

12

13

12. Interior, Church of Reconciliation

13. Brother Roger, writing in his room

Grandchamp

14

5

14. Grandchamp, with chapel to the right
15. Chapel

Missionary Brothers of Charity

16

17

16. Los Angeles, Missionary Brothers with Mother Teresa

17. Brother praying in chapel

Catholic Worker

18

18. Dorothy Day

19

20

19. Woodcut by Fritz Eichenberg

20. Catholic Worker Hospitality Kitchen, Los Angeles, 1972

L'Arche

23

21. Jean Vanier (left) and Raphael
22. Chapel at Trosly—Breuil, France

24

25

23-25. L'Arche Tahoma Hope Community, Tacoma, Washington

Monastic Family of Bethlehem

26. Sisters in chapel, France
27. Sisters in chapel, New York

6

Taizé:
An Ecumenical Community

The community of Taizé is located on a ridge which rises like a cresting wave high above the rolling green fields of Burgundy in France. About ten kilometers to the east lies the little town of Cluny, with the remains of its great monastic church which was once the center of the most powerful monastic movement in Christian history. Taizé represents a fascinating expression of twentieth century monasticism, Protestant in origin but today an ecumenical community.[1]

Roger Schutz

From the beginning the driving force behind Taizé has been its founder and first prior, Roger Schutz. The son of a Swiss father and a French mother, Roger Schutz was born on May 12, 1915 in Provence, not far from Neuchatel. A number of people early in his life taught him to appreciate the inclusiveness of the church. His father, a Protestant pastor, was a prayerful man with an openness towards Catholics. Much the same could be said of his maternal grandmother who inspired him with a love for the Catholic Church as well as a concern for the unfortunate. When Roger was about thirteen he left home for secondary school, living for a time with a Catholic family. His long discussions with his landlady, Madame Bioley, helped him through his own struggle with questions of faith.

In 1936 he went to Lausanne to begin his university studies in theology. He was already interested in monasticism and thinking about some form of Christian community, but his ideas developed slowly. A group of friends with similar interests met regularly for prayer. He was attracted by the idea of starting a house where those interested might gather for prayer and retreats. In 1940 he began looking for one in France, recently defeated by the Germans; the idea was to live a life of work and prayer while assisting those suffering because of the war. In August he crossed into Vichy, France to consider several possibilities. While in the town of Cluny, he found a notice for the sale of a house in nearby Taizé.

After consulting his friends in Lausanne, Roger bought the house. He lived here for two years, helped by his friends in Switzerland, working the land attached to the house, and caring for refugees, many of them Jews fleeing the Nazis. In November 1942 someone denounced him to the Gestapo and he had to flee to Switzerland where he stayed for the remainder of the war.

But his ideas on community continued to develop. In April of 1943 he completed his thesis: *The ideal of the monastic life before Saint Benedict and its conformity to the Gospels.* He had met several others with similar interests. One was Max Thurian, also a young theologian, another was Pierre Souvairan, studying agriculture. They lived with Roger in his flat in Geneva. They were soon joined by a fourth, Daniel de Montmollin. Together they lived a common life, but one that was open to the many students, refugees, workers, and other friends often to be found at the flat. This small group was to become the nucleus of Taizé.

The Taizé Community

After the liberation of France in 1944 Roger and his first three brothers returned to the house at Taizé. Their life began to take on the pattern of prayer, hospitality, and service which would become characteristic of the community. Three times a day they gathered for prayer in a small chapel in their house.

The beatitudes were central to their way of life. Roger gave them a simple rule, derived from that of the Veilleurs.

> Throughout your day let work and rest
> be quickened by the Word of God.
> Keep inner silence in all things
> and you will dwell in Christ.
> Be filled with the spirit of the Beatitudes:
> joy, simplicity, mercy.[2]

The little community opened their home to children displaced by the war. They also ministered to a group of German prisoners of war whose presence in the region was not appreciated and helped the local inhabitants to improve their farming methods. The first French brother, Robert, joined in 1948. A petition to use the vacant parish church of Taizé, a beautiful but long neglected Romanesque structure, was returned with the signature not of the local bishop but of the nuncio in Paris, Angelo Roncalli, later to be elected John XXIII.

On Easter Sunday, 1949, the brothers of Taizé, now numbering seven, gathered in the church to make a public profession. Each promised to live in communion with his brothers, to renounce all ownership, to practice celibacy, and to follow the decisions of the prior so that they might be of one heart and one mind. As the community continued to grow, the need for some written guidelines became more evident. Thus in the winter of 1952-53, Brother Roger took some time out for silence and prayer and composed the *Rule of Taizé*.[3]

The rule is more a description of their life and exhortation than a set of regulations. Its preamble makes clear that it is not to be understood as a law which dispenses one from the responsibility of discovering anew God's will. Organized into four sections, it describes the activities of the community, its spiritual discipline, its commitments or vows, and some practical instructions on brothers outside Taizé, new brothers, and guests.

The spirituality of Taizé represents an open monasticism which has managed to unite a life of contemplation and liturgical prayer with a deep commitment to the work of reconciliation, in the church and in the world. Prayer, both personal and liturgical, holds pride of place. In spite of the tens of thousands of people who come to Taizé every year, the monks are careful never to forget their community life and their personal spiritual journeys. Their rule counsels an interior silence which nourishes a life of contemplation and makes possible the encounter with God.

Today the community numbers about ninety monks. Since 1966 a community of Catholic sisters, the Sisters of St. Andrew, have been associated with Taizé. They live in a neighboring village and assist with the welcome.

Church of Reconciliation

To accommodate the growing crowds of visitors, the large Church of Reconciliation, designed by one of the brothers, was financed and built by a German reconciliation movement. It was dedicated in 1962. On entering the visitor sees large panels with an inscription in several languages: each reads, "Be reconciled, all you who enter here: parents and children, husbands and wives, believers and those who cannot believe, Christians and their fellow-Christians."

The church, a large, concrete structure, looks from the outside more like a slightly misshapen airplane hanger than a monastic church. But over the years it has been transformed into a marvelous space for silent prayer and communal worship. In 1971 the front wall of the church was made movable, so that the church itself could be expanded with a huge tent to accommodate the summer crowds.

The body of the church is dark, but pierced by shafts of colored light from stained glass windows along one wall, behind the sanctuary, and at the juncture of the standing walls and the roof. Oil lamps illumine icons at various places. The cross of Taizé stands to the right of the sanctuary. The central section of the church, marked off by low planters, is reserved for the brothers, while the rest of the floor space and two raised side areas accommodate the many guests. The sanctuary is brightly colored and lit with candles.

Liturgy

The life of the Taizé community revolves around the liturgical prayer or office. Three times a day, at 8:00 in the morning, at 12:20, just after noon, and at 8:30 in the evening bells call all, monks and visitors, to the Church of Reconciliation for prayer. The office is designed so that all can participate. Visitors approaching the church are greeted by young people holding signs which say simply, "silence." The church is a place of prayer. People sit on the floor or kneel on little wooden prayer benches. Some prostrate themselves on the floor. Shortly before the beginning of the office, the brothers begin filing into the church, dressed in the white hooded habits they wear for liturgy and prayer.

Suddenly a joyous chant fills the church. The office has begun. More simple than the traditional office, it consists of a psalm which is sung, a reading from Scripture, usually in several languages, followed by a long period of silent reflection. Petitionary prayer follows the period of silence. Usually the response is *Kyrie eleison,* Lord, have mercy. A hymn, often one of the "canons" or chants, sung in French, German, English, Italian, and Spanish, conclude the common prayer. In the evening, many people together with some of the brothers remain in the church and continue singing for another hour or two. The Eucharist is distributed after morning prayer except on Sundays, when it is celebrated for all those present.

The chants of Taizé, many of them written by Jacques Berthier, a organist in Paris, have become famous worldwide. Simple in form, one or two lines, often in Latin, repeated over and over, they both invite newcomers to participate and move them into prayer.[4] *Veni Sancte Spiritus. Laudate Omnes Gentes. Crucem Tuam Adoramus Domine. Surrexit Christus Alleluia.* They are sung in a dark church, lit only by candles. The readers use flashlights.

At the end of each week the community celebrates a little Easter, beginning with the prayer around the cross on Friday evening, a celebration of the resurrection in the Saturday evening office, and the Sunday Eucharist. The tradition of the prayer around the cross originated in Eastern Europe where Christians, forbidden to gather publicly for prayer, would come together in someone's home and pray around a cross placed on the floor.

At Taizé, the cross with an icon of the crucified Savior is

brought from its usual place at the front of the church into its center after the evening prayer and laid on the floor, surrounded by candles. While the entire congregation fills the church with song, people begin approaching the cross, stepping over the small planters which separate the section reserved for the brothers from the rest of the church. In twos and threes, they kneel before the cross, kissing it or praying with their heads resting upon it. Others wait their turn in line, kneeling. It is always a moving experience to see this crowd of people from all over the world, coming without hesitation to express publicly and before strangers their own faith in the healing power of the crucified Christ. Often they remain praying quietly in the church until late in the night.

Human Solidarity

Prayer and human solidarity go together at Taizé like breathing in and out. From the earliest days, when Brother Roger gave shelter to Jewish refugees fleeing from the Nazis, Taizé has been attentive to victims of poverty and injustice. In the 1950s, as soon as the number of brothers had reached twelve, some of them went to live in places of suffering and division, to be witnesses to peace and to share their lives with the outcasts of society. Today, part of the community lives in small groups, known as "fraternities," in places such as the northeast of Brazil, Kenya, Korea, and Bangladesh. A fraternity is also located in New York's "Hell's Kitchen," a diverse neighborhood of central Manhattan where many Hispanics live. From there, the brothers have travelled to over sixty cities in North America to help create links between Christians committed in different ways.

Brother Roger himself goes each year to spend time in a part of the world where people are undergoing difficulties. While there, he often writes an open letter to the young on topics that will be discussed in the meetings in Taizé and elsewhere during the coming year. He visited Chile just after the coup d'etat there, and has spent time in the slums of Calcutta as well as in South Africa, Lebanon, Haiti, sub-Saharan Africa suffering from drought, and Ethiopia. He also goes to Eastern Europe each year, where Taizé brothers have had relationships with the young and the not-so-young for over twenty-five years.

Reconciliation

"Ecumenism" is not a word heard very often in Taizé, and yet, at the very heart of Taizé's vocation is the call to be a "parable of community," a tiny sign to make visible the Gospel's call to reconciliation. By bringing together brothers from different Christian traditions, Taizé is, by its very existence, a sign of reconciliation between Christians separated by old and new divisions. From the beginning the community brought together brothers from the Reformed and Lutheran churches. Anglican brothers came in the sixties, and the first Roman Catholic brother in 1969, with the approval of the president of the French bishops' conference. The presence of Roman Catholic brothers led the community to speak out more clearly on the gifts of that tradition: the Eucharist as a sign and source of the unanimity of the faith, and the ministry of a "universal pastor."

On the level of theological ecumenism, Brother Max Thurian, one of Brother Roger's first companions, has done significant work. In addition to his numerous books and articles on the liturgy, Eucharist, marriage, celibacy, and Christian unity, Brother Max chaired the committee which did the final editing on the World Council of Churches 1982 convergence text, *Baptism, Eucharist and Ministry.*[5]

Perhaps the best expression of the Taizé community's vision of the ecumenical vocation can be found in some words spoken to the brothers by Pope John Paul II during his visit to Taizé in October 1986. "By desiring to be yourselves a`parable of community'," said the Pope, "you will help all whom you meet to be faithful to their church affiliation, the fruit of their education and their choice in conscience, but also to enter more and more deeply into the mystery of communion that the Church is in God's plan."

In recent years, Brother Roger has often insisted on the necessity for Christians, while ecumenical agencies continue to search for a visible, institutional reconciliation, to achieve an inner reconciliation within themselves. They should dispose themselves inwardly day after day to trust in the mystery of faith in its entirety, and not just those parts with which they happen to agree.

Although reconciliation between Christians is at the heart of Taizé's vocation, however, the brothers insist that this is never an end in itself. Its purpose is to make it possible for Christians to be a leaven of peace and reconciliation throughout the human family. The fact that today the community includes brothers not just from Europe but from Africa, Asia, and America as well, is an important sign in this respect. Brother Roger has emphasized for many years that ecumenism has to reach beyond its western origins and find ways of linking Christians of the prosperous northern countries with their brothers and sisters in the impoverished southern hemisphere.

Taizé and the Young

In the sixties, young adults started coming to Taiz as a place of pilgrimage. The community began to build simple accommodations to house them, and their numbers continued to grow. In 1970, Brother Roger launched the idea of holding a "Council of Youth." At a time when the young were falling prey to discouragement and leaving the church, the council of youth awakened new hope by offering them a concrete way of taking part in the reconciliation of Christians and in building peace on earth. When it finally opened in 1974 after four years of preparation, the opening celebration brought some 40,000 young people to Taizé.

The council of youth gradually evolved into a pilgrimage of reconciliation involving young adults from across the world. In 1982, during a stay in Lebanon, Brother Roger proposed a "pilgrimage of trust on earth." He did not have in mind an organized movement centered on Taizé, but a call to young and old to set out in their own situations, by very concrete commitments, to be bearers of peace and reconciliation in the church and in the world. This "pilgrimage of trust" involves as well the creation of links between committed people on every continent through visits, letters, and the bimonthly *Letter from Taizé*.

As stopping points on this pilgrimage, Taizé organizes meetings that bring together thousands of young people. They pray in the cathedrals and are hosted by parishes and congregations in large cities such as Montreal, New York, Washington, Madrid, Lisbon, Dublin, and Brussels. Each year, 20,000 to 30,000 attend a European meeting, usually in Paris, Rome, London, Barcelona, or Cologne. There have also been two large intercontinental meetings in Madras, India, and East-West meetings in Yugoslavia and Hungary. In 1989, to mark the changes taking place in Europe, the European meeting was held in Wroclaw, Poland.

At times Brother Roger makes public gestures for peace in the name of the young. To emphasize their symbolic character, he often is accompanied by children from every continent. Thus he met the American and Soviet ambassadors during a meeting held in Madrid, and on two occasions met with UN Secretary General Perez de Cuellar, bringing to him the suggestions of the young regarding world peace. In 1988 he was awarded the UNESCO Prize for Peace Education in Paris.

Today, during the summer months, between two and four thousand visitors, mostly between 18 and 25, come to Taizé each week. They take part in week-long intercontinental meetings centered on the sources of faith, and participate in the common prayer of the community. These pilgrims come from close to a hundred different nations.

Conclusion

Rather than being either Protestant or Catholic, Taizé today in a real sense is both. It is a genuinely ecumenical community.

As a monastic community, Taizé has played an important role in bringing a new awareness of contemplative prayer and a sense for liturgy, both to the reformed churches of Europe and to the thousands of young people from all the churches who have spent time at Taizé. It has also provided the Catholic Church with a new vision of unity.

The many young people who come to Taizé experience reconciliation and communion with Christians from different traditions in a very practical and personal way. For them, this personal experience is far more important than structural and institutional concerns. Yet at the same time it remains true that for many of them, Taizé brings about a discovery of the Gospel which cannot be separated from the church which proclaims and lives it.

At Taizé it becomes clear that reconciliation must mean more than the reconciliation of churches. It must also overcome the divisions between peoples. Human solidarity is seen as a sign of authentic prayer and contemplation.

Brother Roger has repeatedly emphasized the "provisional" quality of a life rooted in contemplation.[6] The brothers of Taizé strive to remain open, to be willing to let go for the sake of the unity which still lies in the future. Taizé is not to be a new order, a movement, or a church. It is a "parable of community," a sign at once fragile and powerfully suggestive of what might be.

7.

Contemporary Catholic Religious Communities

A number of currents of renewal were to revitalize Roman Catholic religious communities in the twentieth century. One of the most important was the Second Vatican Council. We need to consider its impact on religious life. But while the Council was the greatest force for renewal, it was not the only one. The impulse to radical discipleship and Christian community has been as evident in the twentieth century as it has been in others.

The years before the Council saw the appearance of a number of religious communities which have sought to combine a contemplative life with a profound solidarity with the poor. We will consider two of them, the Little Sisters of Jesus and the Missionaries of Charity. Then we will look at the Bethlehem community, a community which has given a new witness to the monastic vocation with a strong eremitical dimension. Finally, we will review briefly the impact of the Council on Catholic religious communities in general.

The Little Sisters of Jesus

In 1916 a French hermit, living deep in the solitude of the Sahara, was killed by some tribesmen in revolt against the French. The hermit, Charles de Foucauld, had hoped to be joined by others who would live with him a ministry of prayer and presence. They never came. But some years after his death, a number of communities, the Little Sisters of Jesus among them, were established which drew their inspiration from him. Foucauld's story is a strange one; though it has been enormously influential, even today, it still remains relatively unknown.[1]

Charles de Foucauld

Born in Strasbourg in 1858 of an upper class family, Foucauld was orphaned at the age of four and raised in the home of his grandfather. His early years were distinguished only by his self-indulgence. He attended the military academy of Saint-Cyr, finishing near the bottom of his class. In 1881 he was forced to resign his commission for refusing to give up his mistress when his regiment was transferred.

He rejoined his regiment a few months later to help suppress a native revolt in French Algeria, showing for the first time his courage and capacity for leadership. Restless, he resigned again in 1882. He returned to Africa and after some preparatory studies in Algiers, he spent two years traveling through Morocco, still unknown and hostile towards most Europeans, in the company of a rabbi. His observations won him honors in 1885 from the Geographical Society of Paris. They were published in 1888.

But Foucauld was not able to exploit the opportunities his scholarship had opened up. The Sahara and the simple faith of its Moslem tribesmen had made a deep impression on him. A friendship in Paris with the Abbé Huvelin helped him return to the faith he had given up as a youth. The turning point was a confession he made to the Abbé in October of 1886. From that moment he was utterly convinced of God's existence and determined to devote himself to God alone.

It took Foucauld some time to find his precise vocation.[2] In 1890 he entered the Trappist monastery of Notre Dame des Neiges in the mountains of the South of France. He wanted to live in utter simplicity, and after a few months transferred to a much poorer and more rigorous monastery at Akbès in the north of Syria. The monastery at Akbès was little more than a collection of farm buildings and huts.

But still he was restless. A vigil in the hovel of a Arab

laborer who had just died showed him the clear contrast between the relative wealth of the monks and the utter poverty of the laborer and his family. He began to dream of a congregation of his own, to be called the Little Brothers of Jesus, and in 1896 drafted a rule describing their life. They would live the life of Jesus in Nazareth, but their Nazareth would be among the contemporary poor. Like the poor, they would support themselves by doing manual labor. But their life would be also contemplative, focused on the presence of Jesus in the word of the Gospel and in the Eucharist.

He began to seek release from the Trappists. He was sent to another monastery at Staoueli in Algeria, and then to Rome to prepare for ordination. In 1897 he left the Trappists and returned to the Holy Land, living for two years as a hermit, first at Nazareth where he worked as a handyman for the Poor Clares, then at Jerusalem. During this time he continued to work on his rule, now in a second draft. He now envisioned small communities of brothers which would be known as "fraternities." They would live among the most poor.

In 1901 he went to France and was ordained. Then he returned to the Sahara, settling first at Beni-Abbès near the border of Algeria and Morocco. He remained there for four years, praying before the Blessed Sacrament which was always exposed, welcoming travelers, hoping to be joined by other brothers who never came.

In 1905 he moved much deeper into the Sahara, building his hermitage outside the village of Tamanrasset in the country of the nomadic Touareg, a Berber people. To the natives he was a "marabout" or holy man. He had a great desire to bring Christ to the Moslem peoples, but by living the Gospel rather than preaching it. Thus his ministry was one of prayer and presence. He made friends with his neighbors, studied their language, compiled a dictionary of Touareg, and prayed in his tiny two room hermitage. In 1916, during a period of local unrest, he was killed by some hostile tribesmen; he died instantly, shot through the ear by a fifteen year old.

Foucauld left behind him drafts for two rules, one written in 1896 at Akbès and another drawn up at Nazareth in 1899. A later text outlining his vision was dated 22 July 1905, from Tamanrasset. Though he experimented with different ideas, he returned at the end to the idea of small groups, in order to live in real poverty. He saw communities without enclosure, living among the poor, sharing their social condition and status, doing manual labor to support themselves, gathered in small fraternities of three to five, each with a chapel at its center for prayer and adoration. Neither contemplative or active religious in the traditional sense, their apostolic work was to prepare others for the Gospel, or "pre-evangelization." His model was the hidden life of Jesus in Nazareth.

He did not live to see the communities of Little Brothers and Little Sisters he had dreamed about. But his vision of a new kind of religious community was soon to be realized, not just by several communities which would look to him for their inspiration, but by others as well whose solidarity with the poor, contemplative life, and ministry of presence he had sketched in his journals and modeled in his own life.

The first biography of Foucauld was published in 1921.[3] Others followed and his fame grew. Several men under the leadership of René Voillaume organized themselves as the Little Brothers of Jesus in 1933 at El Abiodh, Algeria.[4] They were recognized as a religious congregation by the church in 1936. That same year, a congregation of women, known as the Little Sisters of the Sacred Heart, was established at Montpellier in France. After the Second World War, during which time the Brothers were disbanded for military service, the Little Brothers grew rapidly, though they have remained a small community.

The Little Sisters of Jesus

A third congregation, *Les Petites Soeurs de Jésus,* was founded in September 1939 at Touggourt, Algeria by Little Sister Magdeleine of Jesus. The first two sisters, Little Sister Magdeleine and Little Sister Anne, had spent a year with the White Sisters at their novitiate near Algers. On September 8, 1939 they made their profession. In October they established the first fraternity of the Little Sisters of Jesus among the tent dwelling nomads of the Sahara at Touggourt. Living like the nomads themselves, they were determined to live out Foucauld's vision.[5]

In 1940 the first five novices joined the community, making most of their novitiate at le Tubet in Aix-en-Provence. The house at le Tubet was to become the mother house. In the years following the war many women came to join the congregation. Though the congregation would maintain a particular dedication to those who lived in Islamic countries, it took on a universal character as the sisters established fraternities around the world. By the mid fifties they were present on five continents. In March 1964 the Little Sisters of Jesus were recognized by Rome as a pontifical congregation with its general fraternity in Rome. By then there were some seven hundred and forty-five professed sisters and over one hundred and fifty novices from forty-six different nationalities. In 1982 their number was about 3500.

A candidate for the community spends a number of months of probation before making a year's postulancy and another year of novitiate. After first vows, she spends four or five years in a fraternity, and a year studying theology. Then she goes to the general fraternity at Tre Fontani in Rome for her final profession.

To maintain the utter simplicity of their life, the Little Sisters live in fraternities consisting of two to six members. In a more activist age, their life may strike some as strange. Like that of Charles de Foucauld, their vocation is one of prayer and presence. Their fraternities are as poor as the isolated areas and neighborhoods in which they are located. Each is simply furnished. At the center of each is a chapel.

In a typical fraternity, the sisters gather in the chapel for morning prayer and meditation after rising early. Then they join a local parish congregation for the liturgy. After breakfast, they go to their various jobs. At the end of the day they return to the chapel for an hour of adoration before the exposed Blessed Sacrament. After supper and some time for recreation and study, they gather again for night prayer before retiring. Most of the little sisters today wear denim skirts and blouses, usually with a simple wooden cross with a heart. Their life is contemplative, but their monastery is the everyday world of the poor.

The sisters do not want to take jobs or even ministries, such as teaching, which will raise them above the poor among whom they have chosen to live. They have established fraternities among the nomads of the Sahara and in the slums of Santiago in Chile. They have taken care of Lepers in Cameron, lived with the natives in Alaska and with Indians in Peru. There is a fraternity in the Arab quarter of Jerusalem. In the United States they have six communities. Like the poor, they choose whatever work is available locally. They may work in factories, sometimes joining the necessary unions. In agricultural areas they work in the fields. Some have travelled as gypsies or as circus workers. They have washed dishes, cleaned buildings, worked in hospitals and fast food restaurants.

Sharing the lives of the poor, the unevangelized, and the de-Christianized is an essential dimension of their life. They try always to be good neighbors, to welcome those who visit them, to make friends with them. Simple acts of kindness bond them to their neighbors, visiting their homes, caring for a sick child, taking an interest in their concerns. Always the model is the hidden life of Jesus at Nazareth.

The Missionaries of Charity
Mother Teresa

Agnes Gonxha Bejaxhiu was born in Skopie, Albania, now part of Yugoslavia, on August 27, 1910. She became interested in India while she was in school; she was a member of a sodality which regularly received letters from Yugoslav Jesuits working in Calcutta. When she was eighteen she joined a missionary order, the Sisters of Loreto, entering the community in Dublin and being sent almost immediately to India where she made her novitiate in Darjeeling. In 1931 she took her vows, choosing the name by which the world would know her, Teresa.

From 1928 to 1948 she taught at St. Mary's in Calcutta, serving for a while as principal. St. Mary's was an upper class high school for Bengali girls, a beautiful complex in the midst of the squalor of the city. Attached to it was an orphanage for the children of the poor. In 1941 Mother Teresa and a Belgium priest known as Father Henry began working with the city's poor. As she became more and more familiar with the desperate poverty of the people she began to reevaluate her own life.

In 1946 she asked permission to live outside the community so she could give herself fulltime to working with the poor. She finally received it two years later.

On August 18, 1948, the year after India achieved its independence, she left Loreto, putting aside the community's black habit and dressing herself in a simple white sari with a blue border and cross on the shoulder. She went to Patna to spend several months with the Medical Missionary Sisters, an American congregation, for some basic medical training. When she returned to Calcutta she opened a small school in Moti Jheel, a slum adjacent to the Loreto convent, and began tending the sick. Soon she was joined by two of her former students, Subhasini Das and Magdalene Gomes, now known as Sister Agnes and Sister Gertrude. The new community was known as the Missionaries of Charity. They lived in an unused room in the home of Michael Gomes, a Bengali Catholic. As more young women joined them, the community gradually took over one whole floor and most of the roof of the Gomes' home.

The Missionaries of Charity.

In the years that followed the sisters began a number of ministries which have become characteristic. Because of the many lepers in Calcutta they established a leper colony near the city known as Shanti Nagar or City of Peace. The inability of the city's hospital to care for the dying destitute led to the foundation of Nirmal Hriday, the Place of the Pure Heart, set up in 1954 in Kalighat, a vacant building next to the Hindu Temple of Kali. A children's home, Shishu Bhavan, was founded to care for the infants left to die on the streets.

The story of the sisters is well known.[6] Their life is motivated by a mysticism of service which recognizes Jesus present in the broken bodies of the poor as well as in the bread and wine of the Eucharist. In addition to the traditional three vows of poverty, chastity, and obedience, they take a fourth vow of charity. Their day begins at 4:30 with meditation and then Mass. Before they leave for the day's work they do their daily washing and cleaning. The day is spent working with the poor, ministering to the sick, gathering the dying from the streets, teaching the children. At noon they break for prayer, and in the evening they spend an hour in adoration.

Their poverty is particularly severe. Two saris, a bucket, a piece of soap, and a straw mat constitute the worldly possessions of each sister. As the community has spread around the world, Mother Teresa has been criticized for not allowing the sisters to adapt their way of life more to local conditions. Still they have continued to grow. Today the number of sisters is about 2500.

For Mother Teresa, the support that contemplative communities give to the work of caring for the poor through their prayer is particularly important. In 1976 she established a second, contemplative community of sisters in New York. Called the Sisters of the Word, their life is one of contemplation and adoration before the Eucharist, but it still allows a few hours for direct service of the poor. She has also established links between other contemplative communities and the communities of her sisters.

The Missionary Brothers

The story of the Missionary Brothers of Charity is much less familiar. As her own community grew, Mother Teresa found a number of young men attracted to the work. They came to help as volunteers. In March 1963 she established a community for brothers; it became the order of the Missionary Brothers of Charity.

In 1964 Ian Travers-Ball, an Australian Jesuit, came to India to work with the brothers as part of his Tertianship. He had wanted to work with the poor, and felt himself called to remain with the brothers. He received permission to leave the Jesuits and join the community. Taking the name of Brother Andrew, he became the superior of the brothers.

Like the sisters, the brothers increased rapidly. They taught in the slums of Calcutta, opened a number of homes for the sick and the dying, a home for handicapped and retarded children, and several centers for lepers. The brothers often work with juvenile delinquents, the homeless, and drug addicts. Their communities began to appear around the world. They had five houses in Viet Nam and Cambodia.

After the fall of Saigon a group of the brothers who were there came to Los Angeles to open the first house in the United States. They found a place to live in a poor neighborhood not far from downtown. They set to work immediately, making the place habitable, and ministering to the homeless, the addicts, the abandoned old people in cheap hotels, and to the many children of the poor of downtown Los Angeles.

Today the brothers have a number of houses in Los Angeles. An initial formation house is for young men attracted to the community; the brothers accept them as "Come and Sees," allowing them to live in the community while they discern the possibility of a vocation to the brothers. There is also a house for the novitiate which last for two years. One house is run as a hospitality home for homeless boys and men not eligible for public assistance. The brothers make a commitment to raise the boys, serving as parents, making sure they get an education. The men, many of whom are sick or handicapped, stay with the brothers from six months up to a year, giving them time to get on their feet. They also run a facility for homeless 18 to 21 year olds; it is a center, open three days a week, where they can come for food, clothes, a shower, and a place to do their laundry.

Some of the brothers work with young people in the city's juvenile detention facilities. One brother begs food for various food distribution centers throughout the city. Another works with convicts who have AIDS.

Without a distinctive habit, the brothers do not stand out as the sisters do. They dress simply, work pants or jeans, a simple shirt with a small crucifix attached, and sandals or running shoes. But their dedication and manner of living is the same.

The brothers' day begins at 5:30. They spend an hour in prayer, celebrating morning prayer from the office, meditating on the Gospel for the day, and doing a half hour of spiritual reading. Then they walk to Mass in their parish church. Most of the day is taken up with their various works. Some are taking classes to prepare them for various ministries. In the evening they pray evening prayer and meditate for an hour prior to dinner before the exposed Blessed Sacrament. Compline or night prayer at 8:30 closes the day and begins the Grand Silence.

There is a spartan quality to their houses. An economy of furnishing, gleaming floors, lots of open space and light, some simple religious art, and the central chapel. Each brother has one day off a week, and one night a week each community does something together, going to a free concert or a museum or perhaps a ball game. One day a month is set aside for more intense prayer.

The key to their vocation is a great desire to find Jesus in the distressing disguises of the poor. Serving the poor rather than poverty of life in itself is their distinguishing characteristic. But their poverty is also quite severe. They live by a radical dependence on divine providence, for their own needs and the needs of those they serve.

Each brother washes his own few clothes by hand. Much of their food comes from government surplus depots or from supermarket goods too old to sell. They sleep on mats rolled out on the floor at night, though many of the communities, recognizing the need for some personal space, now provide the brothers with small private rooms. They are perhaps more flexible in adapting their life than the sisters are. But in trying to live as active contemplatives, they face the same challenge of trying to keep Christ-centered in all they do and of integrating their work and prayer.

There are now almost five 500 brothers, organized worldwide into nine regions. They have houses in Hong Kong, Japan, Taiwan, South Korea, Macao, and the Philippines; they are scattered throughout Central America, South America, and Africa; they are in Los Angeles, London, Paris, and Stockholm. Every six years the "regional servants" or provincials come together with other elected representatives for a General Council. Brother Andrew chose not to run as General at the 1986 chapter and left the community a year later.

There is a contemplative branch of the missionary brothers, called the Missionary Brothers of the Word, established by Mother Teresa in Rome, and an Association of Co-Workers.

The Monastic Family of Bethlehem

One of the most interesting of the new Catholic monastic

communities has the unusual name of the Monastic Family of Bethlehem and the Assumption of the Virgin. The community traces its history to All Saints Days, November 1, 1950, when Pope Pius XII proclaimed the dogma of the Assumption.

Present in the piazza in front of St. Peter's that day were some pilgrims from France. They had come with a Dominican priest, Ceslas Minguet. When these pilgrims heard the Pope stressing that Mary had been taken up body and soul into heaven and thus into the presence of the Divine Trinity, they were struck by a common desire. They wanted to see established communities of silent adoration which would live "on earth as in heaven" the life which the Mother of God now lives in the glory of God.

Their community began on February 2, 1951 when two women began to live a new life of prayer at Chamvres in France. Soon they were joined by others. Within a year there were fifteen of them. They tried to model their life on that of the Virgin Mary; like her, they sought to live each day in obedience to God, cherishing God's word in their hearts, studying it theologically, celebrating it in the liturgy. The sisters were known originally as *les petites soeurs de Bethléem*. Between 1967 and 1979 eleven monasteries were founded.

From the beginning the call to solitude and the contemplative life was very strong. The sisters wanted to combine a vocation to solitude with a liturgical and communal life so that they might abide in the great "Silence of Love" of the Trinity. As early as 1952 they were in contact with the Carthusians and continued to feel themselves drawn towards the spirit and charism of St. Bruno. The hidden life of his disciples seemed the most appropriate ecclesial expression for the life to which they felt called.

In August of 1973 the prior of the Grand Chartreuse offered the sisters the ancient monastery of Currière-en-Chartreuse. It was close by Chartreuse, set in a deep hollow of the mountains, and had been recently renovated. They accepted it and with it the spiritual tradition of St. Bruno, renewing their vows under his patronage. From this time on, each of the monasteries of Bethlehem followed the rhythm of the Carthusian tradition, alternating solitary life in the hermitage with two daily liturgical assemblies and other expressions of a communal life. The members of the community see themselves as a new, twentieth century family of St. Bruno.

The family of communities continued to grow. In October of 1976 the first three brothers received the habit. They began their monastic life at Currière-en Chartreuse. As they began building their monastery at Currière, they too sought to combine the eremitical and communal life in the tradition of St. Bruno.

In 1981 the General Chapter of the Carthusians allowed the Family of Bethlehem, grown to some 200 members, brothers as well as sisters, the right to receive the spiritual paternity of St. Bruno, though they remain a separate community. In June of 1986 the sisters were recognized as a monastic religious institute. Though still under diocesan jurisdiction, the community has sought recognition as a papal institute. Presently there are 350 sisters, with monasteries in Austria, Belgium, France, Israel, Italy, Spain, and the United States. The first American community was established by the sisters at Livingston Manor, New York, in 1987.

The brothers have also been recognized as a monastic union. Though some are ordained priests, the brothers' vocation, like that of the sisters, consists primarily in living out in prayer their baptismal priesthood. There are today twenty-five brothers in two monasteries, one in France and one in Italy. Together the two autonomous communities constitute a monastic family, living the same vocation in their separate monasteries.

The day for the monks and nuns of Bethlehem begins early, and is spent mostly alone:

3:45	rise; lectio divina
4:30	matins and Eucharist (in the church)
7:00	lauds and silent prayer
9:00	terce; meal
9:45	walk
10:15	sext
10:30	study
12:00	manual work until 4:30
3:00	none
4:30	dinner

5:30   vespers (in the church)
7:15   compline; retire

The spirituality of the Bethlehem community is focused on the three divine persons and on the Virgin who has been elevated to the glory of the Father. The members of the community see their vocation as one of stability in a single place where they can open themselves day and night to the loving presence of God. The icon of the Trinity is always to be found at the center of their chapels. The liturgical celebration of the Eucharist, Matins, and Vespers shows the influence of the Christian East. At the consecration all prostrate themselves in a gesture of adoration.

Most of the day takes place in the hermitage or cells. Though the daily order is common, each monk or nun has considerable freedom in choosing the appropriate readings, and following the particular course of study that suits his or her personal journey. In each monastery there are some who don't experience the call to remain always in the solitude of the hermitage; they work outside, but still in silence. The word of God is read, mediated, and studied continually by all.

Each Monday is a "desert day," devoted to total solitude and more intense prayer. A monk or nun might use it to take a long walk in the surrounding country. In the evening the community comes together for the Eucharist.

Sunday is their community day. Most of the offices are celebrated in the church. Often the monks or nuns go for a walk together in the morning. The main meal is taken together in silence in the refectory. Besides the necessary work to build and maintain their monasteries, the community members support themselves by their artistic work, painting icons, making religious statues and pottery.

The monks and nuns of the Family of Bethlehem and of the Assumption of the Virgin live hidden in the desert of their monasteries. What St. Bruno once said of his disciples could be said also of them: "they keep a holy vigil in the presence of the Living God."

Vatican II
And the Renewal of Religious Life

The renewal of religious life in the Roman Catholic Church following the Second Vatican Council is an important part of the story of radical Christian communities. The Council was to touch all areas of Catholic life. The liturgy was reformed and translated into the vernacular. Lay men and increasingly lay women began to take a more active role in the church and its worship. A seismic shift took place in Catholic theology. Critical biblical and historical scholarship opened up new ways of seeing old problems, while the place where theology was done shifted from the seminaries to universities and graduate schools. Theology was thus declericalized.

The Council placed before religious orders and communities a twofold program for the renewal of religious life. Specifically the Council asked for:

> a continuous return to the sources of all Christian life and to the original inspiration behind a given community and an adjustment of the community to the changed conditions of the times.[7]

Religious communities responded generously to the Council's call for the renewal. Within a short span of years, the appearance of religious life in the Catholic Church was to change immensely.

For centuries the lives and daily orders of most religious communities had been basically similar. Awakened by a bell, their members rose early, often at 5:00 a.m., and assembled in the chapel for the office and a half hour meditation. Then they "heard" Mass, ate breakfast together in silence, and returned after breakfast to the chapel for a brief prayer before the Blessed Sacrament before turning to the work of the day. For many communities related to the monastic tradition, work would be interrupted for the other hours of the office. Dinner and supper were usually eaten in silence, accompanied by reading and followed by brief periods of recreation. After Compline or night prayer, the Great Silence began, lasting till after breakfast the next morning.

Thus community life revolved around the poles of the chapel, the refectory, the recreation room, and the bulletin board, all of it completely regulated by the religious superior. But within a few years all this changed. Religious habits or cassocks, early rise, common order, required devotions, community prayer, corporal penances, common rules, cloister, even local superiors in some communities—all institutions and practices unquestioned for years—disappeared.

Genuine renewal, however entailed much more than getting rid of the cassock or shortening the veil. Beyond the pruning away of traditional practices which had lost their meanings, the return to the sources began to change the ways that the various communities perceived their own particular vocations in the church as well as the different gifts each brought to its life.

Many of the monastic communities began to rediscover the contemplative vocation which had first drawn so many men and women into the desert. The Trappists especially began to see the fundamental meaning of their life as contemplative rather than penitential, and adapted it accordingly. Like other monastic communities, they began to question the assumption that being a monk generally meant being a priest. As a result, they did away with the rigid separation between choir monks and the lay brothers.

The Franciscans set out to rediscover the unique spirituality of their founder; they sought to imitate anew the simplicity of his life and his solidarity with the poor. The Jesuits tried to separate the original spirit of St. Ignatius from later attempts to codify it in customs and rules. Studies in the history of the *Spiritual Exercises* led to a rediscovery of the individually directed Ignatian retreat, rather than the preached retreats which had become the practice.

Communities of religious women responded wholeheartedly to the call for renewal and were perhaps most affected by the changes which followed the Council. Many congregations began the long process of rewriting their constitutions, to update them and bring them more clearly into line with the charism of their founders. Teaching sisters who for years had to spend their summer vacations trying to finish their undergraduate degrees were now being sent on for masters' degrees and doctorates by their congregations. Before long many American women religious were better educated than a good number of the church's priests. Many did work in theology and began to teach on university and seminary faculties. Others gave themselves to work with the poor or to parish ministry.

Community itself became a new value as those who sought to live a community life began to reflect on how the dynamics of communal living impacted on personal growth. Institutional concerns and canonical regulations were increasingly seen as secondary to what promoted the growth and maturity of the community members and the mission of the community.

The Council's Decree on the Church in the Modern World, *Gaudium et Spes*, had stressed the right to economic development and the connection between the kingdom of God and the struggle for justice. In response, a number of religious communities began to develop new ministries on behalf of the poor and disadvantaged. Increasingly they came to see working for social change as an intrinsic part of the task of evangelization.

But the choice for a greater solidarity with the poor has been costly. Jesuit father Rutilio Grande, a good friend of Archbishop Oscar Romero, was machine-gunned to death in 1977 in El Salvador. In December 1980 four American women were murdered in the same country by government soldiers; two were Maryknoll sisters, Maura Clark and Ita Ford, along with Ursuline sister Dorothy Kazel and Jean Donovan, a lay volunteer. Between 1975 and 1983 eleven U.S. missionaries have been murdered in Central America, seven of whom were members of religious orders.[8]

On November 16, 1989, a whole community of Jesuits working at the University of Central America in the capital of El Salvador was wiped out when Salvadoran troops from the U.S. trained and equipped Atlacatl Battalion entered their residence at 2:30 am. One of the priests was shot in the house; the rest were dragged outside and murdered. Six Jesuits died, along with their cook and her fifteen year old daughter. In this way, most of the leadership of the Jesuit university in El Salvador was eliminated. The number of Central and Latin American priests, nuns, brothers, Protestant pastors killed since the Council is in the hundreds. If lay leaders are included, the number climbs to the thousands.

The process of renewal was costly in other ways as well. The efforts of the various communities to rediscover the original vision of their founders often called into question "traditional" works, ministries, and practices. The call to adapt to the new circumstances of the times shifted the emphasis in religious life and formation from conformity to external norms and practices to a personal and interior appropriation of the spirit of the community. The spirit once again was considered more important than the letter of the law.

Many religious found the transition to a more interiorized spirituality and the burden of a new freedom difficult. Without the symbols, customs, and external observances which had supported their sense of identity as religious, many found that their lives were no longer recognizably different from others they met "outside," and left religious life. For many others, the new freedom beyond the confines of the seminary, convent, or monastery opened a world of new possibilities. They became involved in new careers; many found themselves in love, and married. Others became frustrated with what seemed at the time to be the slow rate of change or the intransigence of institutions.

The process of renewal was costly, as thousands of religious were dispensed from their vows and left their communities. The Jesuits alone saw their number decrease from 36,000 to 26,000 within a ten year period. In 1962 there were 173,351 sisters in the United States. By 1988 the number had decreased to 106,912. Many communities, particularly of religious women, dwindled in number and were faced with the financial burden of having to support large numbers of retired sisters without the new recruits to contribute their salaries and their lives to keep the community going. Many of them will disappear.

But most communities which have lived through the turbulent period following the Council see it now as a time of purification and growth. They have emerged from it, often with a new sense of their own particular identities, with new and often non-traditional ministries, and with a manner of life which has become at least more humane, if not always more simple.[9]

Changes in lifestyles and ministries have sometimes occasioned a tension between Rome and the religious communities over just how their vocation should be understood. While Rome has stressed the notion of religious life as a consecration, many "active" communities understand themselves as existing for the sake of ministry.[10] As a result of this tension, some contemporary religious communities have moved from a canonical to a non-canonical status.

Consecration implies a life defined and made holy by an offering of self, a renunciation shaped by the vows, distinguished by symbols of the sacred in architecture, dress, and daily order, and safeguarded by a certain distance from the world. Ministry calls for presence and involvement within it. It needs a certain flexibility in regard to practices and structures, a freedom to be able to respond to needs as they become apparent, or to take a prophetic stand when necessary, with all the risks entailed. A minister is always exposed, and thus vulnerable.

The Gospel calls all to minister in various ways for the sake of the kingdom, but a ministry which is not rooted in a life of prayer and worship usually becomes superficial; at worst it can become manipulative and self-serving. Communities which exist for the sake of ministry, particularly those involved in the struggle for social justice, need the witness of contemplative and monastic communities which continue to remind others of the importance of adoration and praise of the mysterious divine presence.

Conclusion

The movement towards solidarity with the poor has been characteristic of a number of religious communities founded in the twentieth century. The example of Charles de Foucauld has been enormously influential. In a real sense, he outlined in his writings and modeled in his own life an open monasticism lived out among the poor. We have seen this open monasticism reflected in different ways in communities such as Grandchamp, Taizé, the Little Brothers and Little Sisters of Jesus, and the Missionaries of Charity.

Grandchamp and Taizé, as specifically monastic communities, are more traditional. But like the communities Foucauld envisioned, they have "fraternities" through which their members can live a ministry of presence among the poor, similar to that of the Little Brothers and the Little Sisters of Jesus. The Missionaries of Charity carry out a more direct ministry to the poor and disadvantaged but are equally contemplative in their way of life.

The Second Vatican Council brought the challenge of renewal to religious communities throughout the Catholic Church. Many have made great efforts to renew their structures, to simplify their lives, and to enter into greater solidarity with the poor. Though the changes which religious communities have experienced in the years since the Council cannot all be laid at the Council's door, nevertheless the Council's impact on religious life has been immense.

The process of renewal has been costly. Religious communities have gone through a process of purification which has left them diminished in numbers, but in many cases strengthened interiorly and challenged by the rediscovery of their foundational charisms. Men and women continue to offer themselves for lives of prayer and service in religious communities, both traditional and newly established.

France especially has seen a number of new monastic communities established in the years since the Council.[11] The Monastic Family of Bethlehem and the Assumption of the Virgin is eremetical in orientation. Others, like the Community of Saint John and the Fraternities of Jerusalem, combine a monastic life with active works. But all of them have in common a life of contemplative prayer which supports a ministry of presence and service to others, particularly the disadvantaged.

Along with prayer, a concern for the poor and disadvantaged has become characteristic of many Christian communities today, lay as well as religious. It is to these lay Christian communities that we now turn.

8

Lay Christian Communities

The twentieth century has seen the formation of a number of new lay communities, both Catholic and Protestant. Like the new religious communities we have considered, many of them see themselves called by the Gospel to solidarity with the poor. Some of them are also prophetic communities engaged in the struggle for social justice. Thus they represent new efforts to live out the Gospel in a radical way. But they are not simply "activist" communities. All of them are faith communities nourished by prayer and worship. Some have a pronounced contemplative dimension. We will consider four of them: the Catholic Worker, Iona, l'Arche, and Sojourners.

The Catholic Worker

On May Day, 1933, in the middle of the Great Depression, an unfamiliar newspaper appeared on the streets of New York. Called the *Catholic Worker*, it was in some ways a Catholic response to the communist *Daily Worker*, and like it, was filled with stories of labor problems, strikes, race relations, and the difficulties faced by the unemployed and the urban poor. Its editor, Dorothy Day, was a thirty-five year old radical journalist, a convert to Catholicism who saw the paper as an instrument for the advocacy of social change.

But not long after the paper appeared, her friend Peter Maurin who had suggested that she start the paper, showed up at her apartment with two hungry, homeless men. She fed them, and before long, other transients were coming for food and shelter. Thus the *Catholic Worker* house became a House of Hospitality, the first of many in a movement which was to spread across the country, providing not just food for the homeless, but also becoming a radical Catholic social force in the midst of a deeply conservative Catholic Church.[1]

Dorothy Day

Born November 8, 1897 in Brooklyn, Dorothy Day showed an interest in writing from her childhood.[2] Her father was a sports writer and she began writing herself at the age of eight. Her family moved to Chicago when she was about nine. She kept diaries, wrote stories, poems, and contributed to a neighborhood newspaper. From reading Upton Sinclair she became interested in the plight of the poor and took time to see first-hand their living conditions in the slums of Chicago's West Side.

By her second year at the University of Illinois she was already writing about social conditions. Dropping out of school, she moved to New York and settled in Greenwich Village. Quickly she became immersed in the radicalism of the Village, writing first for a socialist newspaper and then for a radical magazine called *The Masses*. Though never actually a member of the Communist Party, she aligned herself with the communist movement because of what she recognized as its concern for the poor.

In 1918 she began living with a newspaperman by the name of Lionel Moise. Becoming pregnant, she feared he would leave her and had an abortion in September 1919. Moise left her anyway. Dorothy deeply regretted having had the abortion and remained against abortion until her death. A marriage to Barkeley Tobey lasted only two years. After moving in 1923 to New Orleans she published an autobiographical novel entitled *The Eleventh Virgin*. It was successful enough to have the movie rights bought by a Hollywood studio, giving Dorothy sufficient money to return to New York. She began living with an anarchist named Forster Batterham in 1925, giving birth to a daughter, Tamar Teresa, two years later.

The birth of Tamar was for Dorothy a genuine grace. As a child Dorothy had shown a deep interest in religion. She had been baptized as an Episcopalian at the age of twelve, but had left Christianity behind with much of her past life when she dropped out of college to move to New York. Institutional religion did not seem to show the same concern for the disadvantaged she found in social radicalism. But she found herself increasingly drawn to the symbols and worship of Catholicism. She mentions in her autobiography the early impressions she had of Catholicism, going to Benediction in New Orleans, the comfort of praying a rosary given her by a Russian Jew, watching people stop to pray as the Angelus rang in the evening on Staten Island.[3] Eventually she began going to Mass herself on Sunday mornings. When her daughter was born, she wanted to offer her the faith that she herself was still coming to.

Dorothy had Tamar baptized in March, 1927. Five months later, in December, Dorothy herself was baptized conditionally. The decision was a difficult one. She had known for sometime that her Catholicism would mean the end of her relationship with Forster, and it did. She was all too aware of the shortcomings of the Catholic Church which barely seemed to grasp the radical message of its Lord. But as her feelings settled she knew she was at home. She began reading in the tradition— Augustine, Thomas a Kempis, especially Teresa of Avila— and gradually found a peace which would never leave her.

Dorothy's Catholicism would always be a very traditional one. She accepted the church's structure and authority without question and rarely challenged its hierarchical officials. But her conversion did not mean the end of her social radicalism. Her real problem was finding ways to channel it.

She lost most of her friends after her conversion. In the next few years she tried a number of jobs. She travelled first to Los Angeles and then to Mexico, submitting articles on social problems to *America* and *Commonweal*, both Catholic magazines. But she remained frustrated, looking for some way to combine her new faith with her social radicalism. The answer came in December 1932, with the arrival of Peter Maurin. Shortly after they became acquainted, he suggested that she begin a newspaper for the unemployed.

Peter Maurin

Maurin was an eccentric French Catholic radical and agitator who shouted his ideas to whomever would listen and wrote them down in doggerel verse. In one of his "Easy Essays" he presented a three point program for social change:

> We need round-table discussions
> To keep trained minds from becoming academic.
> We need round-table discussions
> To keep untrained minds from being superficial.
>
> We need Houses of Hospitality
> To give to the rich the opportunity to serve the poor.
> We need Houses of Hospitality
> To bring social justice back to Catholic institutions.
>
> The unemployed need food.
> They can raise that
> In an agronomic university.
> The unemployed need to acquire skill.
> They can do that in a agronomic university.[4]

Maurin's three point program of informed social criticism, houses of hospitality, and communal farms presents in outline form what became the Catholic Worker Movement.

Social Criticism

It is significant that the movement began with a newspaper, for at the heart of the movement is a profound social critique rooted in the Gospel. As Catholic Worker communities spread across the country, so did Catholic Worker newspapers. Cheaply produced, widely distributed, and surprisingly well written, they served to bring a prophetic critique of social issues to the wider church. At the same time, discussions and lectures in Catholic Worker houses, the "round-table discussions" of Maurin's essays, provided the intellectual stimulus which became characteristic of Catholic Worker communities.[5]

In the thirties the Catholic Worker focused on the problems of unemployment, the working class, and the homeless. Its pacifist position during the Second World War cost it dearly in terms of members and communities, but it also foreshadowed and contributed to the development of a much wider Catholic peace movement in the fifties and sixties. Trappist monk Thomas Merton was greatly influenced by Dorothy Day and from his monastery became a leader of the Catholic peace movement. Throughout the seventies and eighties the Catholic Worker addressed the issues of nuclear weapons and the arms industry, American intervention in Latin America, racism, the death penalty, the homeless, the rights of agricultural workers, and women's rights.

Houses of Hospitality

The houses of hospitality, the second point of Maurin's program, provide the opportunity to live out the works of mercy on a daily basis. They began by accident when Maurin brought two homeless friends to Dorothy's apartment for a meal. Of course she fed them. Soon others were coming, for both food and shelter.

The houses of hospitality became centers for the Catholic Worker communities; here their Gospel idealism becomes not theory but praxis. A house of hospitality is many things, but it is first of all a soup kitchen. Even today the name Catholic Worker is for many associated with a line of tattered and hungry men and women, stretching around a storefront and down the block.

As the original community sought to meet the needs of the unemployed in New York, their story, told in their paper, seemed to strike a nerve. Houses of hospitality began to open in other cities. There were thirty-one of them by 1941. An internal debate over pacifism during the Second World War led to a crisis. Many left the movement, some for the military as the U.S. became involved in the war, some for the jobs the war opened up. By January 1945 only ten houses of hospitality remained. The decade after the war was difficult for the Worker, but from twelve houses in 1960 the movement grew again with the revival of the peace movement in the sixties. A book on Catholic Worker houses published in 1988 lists over eighty of them.[6]

A Catholic Worker community today usually consists of a core group of men and women who live together and a much wider circle of volunteers who help with the soup kitchen on an occasional basis and take part in other Worker activities. A unique feature of the Worker is that "guests," some of the homeless themselves, are invited to live in the community. Many hospitality houses are storefront kitchens with offices and bedrooms for community members and guests upstairs. Others are houses, usually in poor neighborhoods. There is a spartan quality to them all—used furniture, walls in need of paint, a few pictures, often of Catholic Worker activities, and some simple religious art. Often a room is set aside of a chapel.

Though each house has a leader, chosen by the members, decisions are generally made—in anarchist fashion—on the basis of a community consensus. The members practice a voluntary poverty. They live off donations, wear secondhand clothes, eat simple food. They refuse to accept money from either the government or the church, to maintain their independence. There is no organization or rule. The Gospel is understood as being at the center of their lives, but each member must discover what it means for him-or herself. Many go to daily Mass.

Communal Farms

Maurin's third point, "agronomic universities," reflects his own peasant idealism. In an industrialized, urban environment he yearned for the simple life of people living together from the fruit of the land. Their farming efforts could also supply the food to be served in the houses of hospitality.

There have been various efforts to establish Catholic Worker communal farms, some successful, others not. The very openness and lack of organization of the movement doomed a number of these efforts at communal agriculture from the start. The communal farms were not able to become the urban utopias Maurin envisioned, but as Mel Piehl points out, they played an important role early in the movement by providing an option for families who found family life in communities of mostly single people difficult to sustain. More specifically, they "probably saved the Catholic Worker from taking on a strictly celibate and formally religious character."[7] There are presently at least seven Catholic Worker farms in the U.S.

Catholic Radicalism

The Catholic Worker became the first expression of American Catholic social radicalism. Many of those who would be its leaders were formed in Catholic Worker communities, among them Ed Marciniak, James O'Gara, John Cogley, and John Cort. O'Gara became editor of *Commonweal* and Cogley, after working for *Commonweal*, went on to become religion editor of the *New York Times*. Others like Michael Harrington, author of *The Other America*, Ammon Hennacy, an anarchist peace activist, and James Forest, who became director of the International Fellowship of Reconciliation, spent time with the Worker before moving beyond it and the Catholic Church.

Today the movement continues to play an important role in calling the larger church to the radical Gospel and in offering an opportunity for those interested to live in community with others. Many young people have been introduced to the Catholic Worker during their high school or university days; some become involved for a summer or for a number of years. Thus it continues to provide a way station or place of refugee for many young people struggling to find their own identities and vocations. Others make the commitment to live the life of the Catholic Worker on a permanent basis.

If the Catholic Worker is an activist Christian community, its spirituality is rooted in the Gospel and especially the Eucharist. Because the meal offered to their guests remains primary, many young people drawn to Catholic Worker communities have come to a rediscovery of the true meaning of the Eucharist. Worker newspapers and brochures still repeat the words of Dorothy Day: "We know Christ in the breaking of the bread. And we know each other in the breaking of the bread." The members of Catholic Worker communities strive to recognize Christ not just in the broken bread of the Eucharist but also in the hungry, the homeless, and the suffering of a broken world.

Dorothy Day died in 1980 at the age of eighty-three, but what she called "the work" continues to go on in the squalid inner cities of contemporary America. In one of the engravings of Fritz Eichenberg, a Quaker artist whose woodcuts began appearing in the *Catholic Worker* in the fifties, Jesus stands hunched and unrecognized in a line of patiently waiting, cold, and obviously poor men and women. It is good to know that in the Catholic Worker houses of hospitality those who slip through the cracks of modern urban life, the homeless and the addicted, the damaged, the deranged, the unemployable, and the abandoned, find a hot meal and a warm welcome.

Iona

The name Iona is linked with the establishment of Celtic Christianity in Britain. An island off the west coast of Scotland, the Irish monk Columba landed here in 536 and built a monastery. In the Celtic style, it was a simple foundation, a few huts made of mud and wattle and an oak church. From Iona other Irish monks travelled across Scotland to the island of Lindisfarne, off the east coast, and from there, evangelized much of the north of England. In 1203 a Benedictine monastery was established on Iona. Restored and expanded in the fifteenth century, the present abbey dates from that time.

During the Reformation the community ceased to exist when its monks were dispersed. Though the church continued to be used for some time for Protestant services, gradually the abbey fell into ruins. Iona's past continued to draw both pilgrims and tourists. In 1910 the sanctuary was restored. But the future of the abbey had to await the arrival in 1938 of a pastor of the Church of Scotland who would undertake both the restoration of its buildings and the reestablishment of a community which would carry on its tradition of worship and work.

Rebuilding Iona

George MacLeod, born June 17, 1895, was a man of great energy and a fertile imagination. Decorated for bravery in the First World War, he afterwards became a pacifist. In 1930 he was appointed as a young pastor to an urban parish in Glasgow, a working class city with a great number of its craftsmen unemployed because of the depression. MacLeod recognized that the church's failure to address the needs of the working class was making it increasing irrelevant. So he found something for his parishioners to do, repairing an old mill near the city. When this project was completed, MacLeod began looking for another task for his craftsmen.

During this same time MacLeod had been giving some thought to the renewal of his church. In a private paper of 1935, he argued that Protestant churches needed to recover the church's catholic heritage as well as to develop new ministries to address the needs of working class people. To do so he proposed the establishment of a "brotherhood within the Church of Scotland, of no permanent vows, into which men of such a mind could come for the first two or three years of their ministry." These ministers would spend the first six months after college in a community; then they would be "drafted out—still as members of the brotherhood—to the congested areas and the housing schemes where they would carry their ideas into practice."[8]

He suggested that his proposed brotherhood be located at Iona, and that it include unemployed craftsmen who would set about a new project, this time restoring the abbey. Thus his two interests came together into what amounted to a Christian community, designed to train urban ministers; it would consist of young divinity students and craftsmen. The Iona Cathedral Trustees approved his plan, some money was raised, and in July of 1938 a group of divinity students and craftsmen took ship for Iona to begin the experiment.

They established themselves for the summer in a number of wooden huts set up next to the ruined abbey and began their life together. Twice a day they gathered in the abbey church for worship. As they worked together to restore the abbey buildings and learned from each other, the corporate nature of Christianity began to become more evident to them. Their community of ministers and working class craftsmen was not unlike a medieval monastery with its choir monks and *conversi* or lay brothers. But the Church of Scotland was not yet ready for this kind of community; initially there was considerable criticism of what was perceived as pseudo monasticism or crypto Catholicism.

The following year the war broke out and plans had to be changed slightly. In the summer period Iona was opened to clergy, ministers in training, and laity for three months of

common prayer, study, and community life. Only the craftsmen would be involved in the building, and a house for the
young ministers was established in Edinburgh. The effect of
this was to involve a wider group from the church in the life of
the community.

The work went on during the war and the community continued to grow. Its style was almost military, with uniform
suits of dark blue for community members and a fixed order
for rising and retiring. Women could not be members. The
first twelve ministers were offered to the Church of Scotland
to work in urban teams. Others continued to come to visit;
they formed the Friends of the Iona Community, entering into
the community's theological reflection and offering their financial support. The community's emphasis on frequent
eucharistic celebrations, its introduction of responses into the
worship, and its mixing of religion and social activism continued to draw criticism. Within the community there were
considerable debates over pacifism.

The dispersion of community members in various urban
ministries led to reflection on what they had in common, and
eventually to a Rule of Life; the Rule specified at least a half
hour each day of private prayer, using the lectionary, an obligation to plan each day before 9:00 a.m. (the result of the
craftsmen's reproach that ministers worked only on Sundays),
and a commitment to try to live on what was determined to be
the average annual income. At the war's end, work had been
completed on the library, chapter house, reredorter, and most
of the refectory and kitchen.

Post-War Years

By 1945 it was apparent that Iona had become more than a
temporary community for ministers in training. Gradually
several degrees or circles of community membership developed.
Many of the Presbyterian ministers who had trained at Iona
continued to follow the Iona Rule of Life to maintain their
membership. An ecumenical dimension was added as men
from other denominations began seeking admission.

The support group known as the Friends of Iona continued
to grow, reaching 5700 by 1947. Community House, opened

on Clyde Street in Glasgow, offered ministers and Friends a place for fellowship, prayer, and political consciousness-raising. Finally, the abbey began to host summer youth camps which brought young people to the island to share in both work and worship, as well as to take summer courses on topics such as prayer, politics, and Celtic church history. Thus the strong social orientation which had characterized the community from its beginning was now expressed in its religious and educational programs; the intention was to bring together spirituality and social action.

The restoration of the abbey was finally completed in 1965. By this time the community consisted of a large group of ministers who had spent their summer months on the island, the craftsmen, and a growing number of laymen. But the community was changing. The first woman, a medical missionary who had worked in North India, was admitted in 1969. An increasing number of visitors were coming to the island. In 1976 the first Roman Catholic joined the community. Though the community has seen considerable change over the years, it has been able to maintain a remarkable continuity.

Today the permanent community at Iona still carries on a daily rhythm of work and prayer. Though its members are both clerical and lay, the current emphasis is much more on new forms of lay ministry. There is some turnover as each member must renew his or her commitment yearly, and some leave because of other responsibilities. The MacLeod Center, built in 1987, symbolizes the community's desire to remain a place of welcome, reconciliation, and prayer.

Ron Ferguson acknowledges that for some the community functions as an alternative church, and yet it remains rooted in the visible church even as it seeks new ways to renew the church's life.[9] Like other Christian communities, it seeks to make the Gospel the pattern for the whole of life. The Celtic monks who first settled the bleak island of Iona would no doubt be in full agreement.

L'Arche

In 1964 Jean Vanier, then a philosophy professor at St. Michael's College in Toronto, invited two mentally handicapped men to live with him in a small house in Trosly-Breuil, a tiny French village about an hour by train north of Paris. At the time Vanier knew far more about philosophy than he did about living with the mentally handicapped. But from his philosophical studies and his own interest in community life he had a deep sense of their particular needs.

He named his house l'Arche, the French word meaning "the Ark." Like Noah's ark, it was to be a place of refuge, at once a fragile community and a sign of hope. Before long young men and women seeking an alternative way of living in a community context began coming to l'Arche. The community at Trosly grew rapidly and new l'Arche communities were established in other countries. Within twenty years there were more than 60. Today there are almost 100 l'Arche communities scattered around the world, including eleven in the United States.

Jean Vanier

Though he was born in Geneva, Switzerland, Jean Vanier is actually a Canadian. His father Georges Vanier was the nineteenth Governor General of Canada. Jean Vanier was educated at the Royal Naval College in England and served afterwards in both the Royal Navy and the Royal Canadian Navy.

Shortly after resigning his commission in 1950, he joined a community of students living in a working area near Paris. The community was directed by Thomas Philippe, a Dominican priest. Its purpose was to bring together students, mostly lay, who were interested in combining their studies with a routine of prayer and philosophical reflection to deepen their own Christian lives. Vanier pursued his own studies at l'Institut Catholique de Paris and in 1962 finished his doctorate, writing on the themes of contemplation, friendship, and justice in the philosophy of Aristotle.[10]

Vanier began teaching in Toronto, but in 1963 he returned to France to visit his friend Thomas Philippe. The Dominican had just begun serving as a chaplain at Val Fleuri, a home for mentally handicapped men in Trosly-Breuil. Though French social agencies were just beginning to take a new look at the way mentally handicapped people were treated, Vanier was deeply moved by the dismal life of the handicapped people he encountered. He has described the lives of two of them, Raphael and Philippe:

> I had met them both in a rather dismal institution: 80 men, more or less profoundly handicapped, living together; no work, locked doors, two big dormitories, a world of sadness, fear and despair. Both Raphael and Philippe had suffered from sickness during the early years of their lives which had caused some brain damage and physical disability. Both were without families; both were then particularly vulnerable, helpless, and at the mercy of administrations who could push them and move them around.[11]

In August 1964 he invited Philippe and Raphael to live with him at Trosly.

Trosly-Breuil

I spent two days at Trosly in the summer of 1988. As its name suggests, Trosly-Breuil is actually two adjacent villages, around which are gathered some twenty-one separate l'Arche foyers or households. These communities include about 200 handicapped people and a similar number of "assistants," men and women, single and married, from various countries and backgrounds who live and work with them. Some of the assistants have made a permanent "covenant" with the community, others stay for periods ranging from several months to a number of years.

The community members at Trosly are scattered in different homes, with a focal point constituted by la Ferme, a courtyard surrounded on three sides by two story farm buildings. A second adjoining complex includes the community's chapel. The chapel looks as though it were once a barn; the building with its high-peaked roof and a great side arch opening into a second nave on the right, makes a perfect church. A few houses up the street is Val Flueri, the old institution for the mentally handicapped which is now one of the foyers of the community. The original l'Arche house is further up the street at a crossroad.

Many of the assistants are quite young. The majority of
them live in the foyers with the handicapped men and women,
joining them in the daily tasks of cleaning the house, shopping
or preparing the food, taking care of the garden. To see them
at table, talking with the handicapped people about the events
of the morning or working with them in the shops, is to
experience a very deep goodness. They dress simply, cotton
slacks or jeans, sandals or running shoes, the women frequently
in long cotton dresses. They receive only a little spending
money, have one free day a week, and one weekend a month
free.

The handicapped men and women are the heart of l'Arche.
In addition to being mentally handicapped, some are physically
handicapped as well. Some could live outside the community
with help. Many could not. At Trosly there is a special home,
la Forestire, for the profoundly disabled, men and women
who cannot walk, speak, or care for themselves. All of them
share the common human need to be loved and cherished.
Many of them have a capacity, usually unrecognized by people
uncomfortable in the presence of the mentally handicapped,
for offering love and tenderness in return.

Some show warmth and affection from the time you meet
them, smiling shyly, welcoming you, or taking you by the
hand to show you something he or she has made. Some are
more reserved, cannot speak properly, or communicate their
feelings verbally. In the eyes of some the pain and rejection
they have so often experienced is evident. But those who have
suffered themselves are often keenly perceptive of the feelings
of others, almost with a kind of affective telepathy. One person,
long associated with the community, told me of being at Mass
one day weeping quietly over some personal sorrow. Beside
her was sitting a man she had long assisted. Never having
outgrown the body he had as a child, he was unable to walk,
speak, or take care of himself. My friend, lost in her own
sorrow, had momentarily forgotten about the man she was
assisting, when suddenly she felt his hand raise up her chin,
while he proceeded to wipe away her tears with his fingers.
"They feel," she said to me simply, by way of explanation.

One night, arriving at a foyer for dinner, I met a young man
with a severe disability. A loss of motor control affected both

his speech and his hands, causing him to jerk about when he sought to express himself. I thought him withdrawn when he refused to shake my hand. But I was a stranger, an outsider. In the community he was clearly at home and comfortable. At dinner he joined in the conversation with much animation, while keeping his eye cocked on me. But after the meal when I had said goodby to the others and was about to leave, he rushed up and grasped my hand in both of his, giving me a very warm farewell.

Spirituality

What is the vision that draws so many men and women to l'Arche and sustains them in the covenant they make to live with the poor in community? Like so many other communities being formed today, life at l'Arche is centered around prayer and the Eucharist, a simple lifestyle, and solidarity with the poor. More than anything else, people are drawn to l'Arche by a basic truth of the Gospel: Jesus identifies himself with the poor and suffering, and when we open ourselves to them, we come to know the peace and presence of Christ. Vanier likes to quote the words of Jesus: "Whoever welcomes one of these little ones in my name, welcomes me; and whoever welcomes me, welcomes the one who sent me" (Luke 9:48).

The beatitudes stand at the center of the spirituality of l'Arche, for they so perfectly encapsulate the Gospel. It is the poor, the suffering, and the merciful who are called blessed, not the powerful or the comfortable. The beatitudes turn conventional values upside down and call those who would be disciples of Jesus to a radically different manner of life. They are to become peacemakers, to accept persecution, to identify with the poor, the hungry, and the suffering. The hidden life of Jesus at Nazareth also provides a continuing subject for contemplation.

Vanier remains a realist. He knows the limitations of the mentally handicapped, the fact that they can demand too much. Working and living with them on a daily basis can lead to frustration and discouragement. But this too is part of what the assistants learn from the handicapped, for the vulnerability of the handicapped helps the clever and the strong to discover and recognize their own weakness. As Vanier has written, "when the handicapped person calls forth our darkness, anger and/or anguish, we discover the truth about ourselves."[12] They call those who follow Jesus, not only to service but to that life in community with others, particularly with those whose brokenness reveals their own, enabling both to come to recognize and experience God's presence.[13]

Such a life is not easy. It must be constantly nourished by prayer and contemplation. One of my first impressions of Trosly was that it was pervaded by a spirit of prayer. We had arrived about five in the afternoon, just in time for the evening liturgy. Since the priest assigned for the day had not shown up to preside, one of the lay assistants led the community in a communion service. The liturgy was marked by a deep peace, even though the readings, homily, and prayer were occasionally accompanied by the inarticulate cries or exclamations of some of the handicapped people present, participating in their own way. That night after dinner we dropped into the chapel for a visit. Two of the assistants, young women, were sitting quietly on the floor before the altar, singing the *Laudate Omnes Gentes*, a canon of praise from Taizé. The beauty of their voices in the stillness of the moment was for us an invitation to join in their prayer.

Besides praise, prayer at Trosly-Breuil is expressed by adoration in the presence of the Eucharist. On the ground floor of one of la Ferme's cottages, really a French farm house built of massive stone blocks, is an oratory, divided in two by a stone wall. An arch is opened into the wall in which the Blessed Sacrament is exposed, lit by six oil lamps. During most of the day and evening, one or two members of the community are present, praying on one of the prayer benches so common in Europe or kneeling with their heads to the floor in adoration. I prayed there with them, grateful for the quiet sanctuary and for the unembarrassed piety of the community members.

The handicapped members also share in the prayer of the community. The day ends with a brief common prayer in each foyer. Those who are able and chose to do so, after careful preparation for their first communion, receive communion at the liturgies. Several, in albs, assist at the altar as liturgical ministers. I was very moved one day at Mass when one of those present, quite handicapped physically as well as mentally, got down on his knees at the consecration with great effort. In all his weakness and pain, he prostrated himself before the eucharistic Christ.

L'Arche Today

L'Arche communities vary in size, from small ones consisting of a single house to very large ones such as Trosly-Breuil. They consist of single and married people, lay and ordained, living in community with the poor. The handicapped people remain at the heart of each community. Each community is independent, led by a "responsible" or coordinator under the supervision of a Board of Directors. The assistants are always willing to call upon doctors, psychologists, and other professionals for help, but feel a special responsibility themselves to keep the communities going. They have discovered the value of structure, to stabilize their communities and to deal with occasional crises.[14]

To become a member of l'Arche, a community must be accepted into the "federation of the Communities of l'Arche." Though the governments of France and Germany allow young people to do two years of community work in lieu of their military service, l'Arche, like other service communities and religious orders, is finding it difficult to attract as many assistants as they need. Here especially the poverty of dependence of those who belong to l'Arche is evident, as is their need to rely on God.

In the United States there are l'Arche communities in Mobile (AL), Erie (PA), Cleveland (OH), Clinton (IO), Washington (D.C.), Syracuse (NY), Ipswich (MA), Missoula (MT), Spokane, Seattle, and Tacoma (WA).

Trosly-Breuil is a predominantly Catholic community. But early in its life l'Arche took on an ecumenical dimension. An Anglican couple, Steve and Ann Newroth, opened Daybreak in 1970, a l'Arche community just north of Toronto, which brings together Anglicans, Catholics, and members of the United Church of Canada. That same year an interreligious l'Arche community was founded in Bangalore, India which includes Moslem and Hindu members. Since then other communities have been established in India. A l'Arche community in Scotland is made up of people from eight different churches who live and pray together in spite of the pain of not being able to share the Eucharist.

The ecumenical and interreligious dimension of communities like this does not make community life—which is always difficult—any easier. Such communities cannot always worship together and sometimes do not even share the same religious symbols through which their identity is expressed. Their very openness can result in even more suffering which cannot be obviated by facile solutions or by slipping into a vague humanism. Yet the members of these communities often receive the inestimable gift of discovering that the Spirit of God is truly at work in the hearts of people from other traditions. This discovery of the Spirit working in the midst of human suffering is truly one of the great gifts of l'Arche. It is a lesson for the whole Church.

Sojourners

The Sojourners Community in Washington, D.C. is a relatively new community. Like the Catholic Worker, it began as a journalistic effort to address critical social issues in the name of the Gospel. Only in this instance, the year was 1971 and the context was the war in Viet Nam, particularly Nixon's invasion of Cambodia, and those involved were not Roman Catholics but evangelical Christians. From the beginning, an evangelical newspaper strongly committed to social justice and critical of American civil religion was something new.

Most of the community's founding members came from conservative evangelical backgrounds.[15] Joe Roos began seeking a more explicit Christian life through his college involvement in an Inter-Varsity fellowship. Bob Sabath traces his Christian faith to a Billy Graham crusade he saw on television during high school. Jim Wallis was raised in the church of the Plymouth Brethren.

But by the time they met as seminarians at Trinity Evangelical Divinity School, a conservative evangelical seminary located at Deerfield, Illinois, a few miles north of Chicago, they had already begun to question the easy identification of American Christianity with the American way of life and its social and political institutions—what they would later call "the American captivity of the church." For Jim Wallis, the stubborn refusal of evangelical Christianity to face up to the evil of racism was the beginning of his radicalization. The Viet Nam war was the catalyst for others.

Wallis is usually considered the principal founder of the community.[16] He spent his first night at Trinity talking with his next door neighbor in the dorm about his disillusionment with the church and his desire for a recovery of the prophetic tradition of the Bible. Soon his room was the meeting place for a group of seminarians with similar concerns. They would gather for long discussions, prayer, and support; they began to publish manifestos, became involved in antiwar demonstrations, and met weekly for worship. Wallis began speaking on other campuses.

By the Spring of 1971 they decided to begin a newspaper which would bring their views to a wider audience. They pooled their resources to come up with $700 to finance the first edition of what they called the *Post-American*, which appeared in the Fall of 1971. On its cover was a picture of Christ taken down from the cross and draped in the American flag. The caption read, "And they crucified him," to make the point that Jesus was being crucified again by an American Christianity captive to its culture.[17] They printed 30,000 copies, only to realize that they had no mailing list, so they set out to distribute it on college campuses, at seminaries and churches, and to whomever might be interested.

Community

By the time the first edition of the paper appeared, the small circle of male seminarians had grown to a group of about thirty people which included single women and married couples. With a focus provided by the paper, they began to talk specifically about some kind of community to enable them to live out a way of life rooted in the Gospel. Wallis describes this in terms of radical discipleship:

We became aware of the broad historical tradition of communities committed to radical discipleship. Just as we were coming to know that we were not alone in the present, so we were realizing that throughout Christian history all of the convictions and commitments that were beginning to shape our life had been present in the lives of other believers before us.[18]

But forming community proved to be more difficult than they expected. In the Fall of 1972 some of the group moved into two adjoining apartments in a low income section of Chicago, close to Lake Michigan. For a while the work of putting out the magazine held them together. But as they talked about what kind of community they would like to build, their relationships with each other began to deteriorate. Ideological differences, interpersonal conflicts, and personal identity issues became increasingly divisive. After two years the effort fell apart and the members of the community scattered.

But the idea of community did not die. A core group around Jim Wallis and Joe Roos gradually began to rebuild their relationships with each other and in this process of reconciliation and healing found again God's grace. In 1975 they moved to the nation's capital to begin again as a community. In the group were eighteen adults and two infants. They chose Washington in part because the contacts they had been developing through the paper were mostly in the East. Again they chose to live among the poor, settling in a couple of old houses in Columbia Heights, a poor Black neighborhood just east of the White House.

Sojourners

With the move came a new name, Sojourners, for both the magazine and for the community. Based on Hebrews 11 which speaks of the People of God as strangers or exiles on earth, the name Sojourners expresses the distance that the community feels between itself and American society. The community is a resistance community. But the change in name also reflects the growing maturity of the community. Where the name *Post-American* suggested an alienation from traditional American institutions, whether political or religious, the change to *Sojourners* reflects a more positive vision which includes a rebuilding of the church, particularly on the local level.

Living in inner city Washington was difficult, but the community prospered. As of 1987, the community included thirty adults and ten children, living in a variety of houses and apartments in Columbia Heights. They see themselves as called to reflect the Kingdom of God in the historical circumstances of their everyday lives. That means for all of them a commitment to social justice.[19]

The community's lifestyle is simple, decisions are shared, funds are held in common. While the members are accountable to one another, the community has recognized five of their members, both men and women, as pastors. In the early days leadership was implicit rather than explicit, but this ultimately proved less than adequate; they found that implicit leadership could be manipulative because the leaders could not be held accountable. The presence of children has presented a special challenge. This, and a strong commitment to feminism, has led to an emphasis within the community on co – parenting. Each year the community makes a retreat together.

The community supports a number of ministries, both local and directed towards the wider church. Ministries to their inner city neighborhood include a tenant organization, a food distribution program, support groups for mothers, nutrition education, and special programs for children. Outreach ministries include the magazine, a peace ministry which addresses peace and justice issues, a speaking and teaching ministry, a resource center, and an internship program.

The *Sojourners* magazine has become one of the most respected and widely read in the United States. Its combination of concern for social justice with evangelical faith has made it difficult to categorize. One finds in its pages not just articles on nuclear issues, the peace movement, feminism, urban poverty, torture and political repression in Third World countries, racism in South Africa and in the U.S., but also on sexual responsibility, right to life for the unborn, prayer, solitude, and contemplation. The only thing predictable about the magazine's point of view is its commitment to social justice, the expression of its fidelity to the Gospel.

Both the community and the magazine have become ecumenical. Wallis acknowledges the influence of Catholicism, "especially the gospel radicalism of the Catholic Worker and the powerful tradition of Catholic spirituality and contemplative prayer."[20] Mainstream Protestant, Anabaptist, and charismatic traditions have also contributed. On Sunday evenings the community gathers at the Sojourners Neighborhood Center for worship. Eucharist is celebrated with a loaf of bread and a simple ceramic cup. The service is open to all comers and generally draws about seventy-five people. For this Gospel community which has given such a powerful witness to justice issues, worship remains central.

Conclusion

The communities we have considered in this chapter represent contemporary expressions of the impulse to radical discipleship. They are communities of lay men and women, both single and married, rather than religious or monastic communities. Each has attempted to make possible for its members a way of life rooted in the Gospel.

Like other Christian communities before them, these are alternative communities. Besides having a common commitment to prayer, worship and life in common, they have shared a commitment to living in solidarity with the poor. This latter commitment entails a simple lifestyle. It also means living and working with the poor and the disadvantaged, as well as action on behalf of justice. In this sense they have been social justice communities, and have in different ways challenged both their societies and their churches by attempting to live out the radical challenges of the Gospel.

Catholic Worker communities have fed and clothed the poor and homeless of the inner cities since the beginning of the movement. The members of Sojourners have taken on a particular responsibility to assist the urban poor among whom they live. Both communities carry on as well a prophetic ministry on behalf of peace and justice through their publications and a personal involvement of their members. Civil disobedience and protest has led to arrests and sometimes to prison terms. The Iona community has tried to develop new ministries, both ordained and lay, for tomorrow's church. L'Arche allows handicapped people to live, not as rejected outcasts but as persons loved and valued by sisters and brothers in communities around the world.

These communities we have considered are not the only ones. The Church of the Savior in the Washington, D.C., has carried on a Gospel ministry for many years which seeks to create community with the poor of the inner city and bring about social change. And there are many others.

As Jim Wallis has said, "The oldest and best traditions of the church demand that the gospel be proclaimed and lived in the midst of the suffering world, and that those who would follow Jesus Christ be particularly sensitive to the poor and the oppressed. A commitment to social justice is simply a consequence of faith in Jesus Christ."[21] This critical, prophetic commitment and the solidarity with the poor which it entails is characteristic of those contemporary Christian communities which are attempting to live the fullness of Christ's Gospel in our own day.

Church leaders, with Iona Abbey and Mull in background. The tall man in the center is Rev. George MacLeod.

9

BCCs and Covenant Communities

In addition to the communities we have considered in the last three chapters, the twentieth century has also seen an increasing number of lay Christian movements which have an important community dimension. Their vitality suggests that the need for a communal expression of the Christian life is still deeply felt.

Italy has a number of these community movements. One of the oldest, the Focolare movement (the name means "hearth" or "family fireside") traces its beginning to a decision made in 1943 by its founder, Chiara Lubich. In the midst of the destruction caused by the Second World War, Chiara decided that she would focus her life entirely on the Gospel. A group of her friends joined her. Today Focolare is an international movement with over a million members. Another Italian movement, the Roman community of San Egidio, has expanded into Belgium and Germany and has over 3,000 members. A third, *Comunione e Liberazione*, founded in 1954 by the Italian priest Luigi Giussani, is a growing movement with a concern for conservative politics. Its international magazine includes an English-language edition, *30 Days*.

In Latin America, the renewal of the Catholic Church following the Second Vatican Council was to lead to the establishment of basic Christian Communities throughout Latin and Central America and in other Third World countries.

From the Catholic charismatic renewal which began in 1967 a number of "covenant" communities have emerged in the United States. Reaching France in 1971, the renewal has led to a number of charismatic communities there as well.

In this chapter we will focus on two of these movements, the covenant communities in the United States and France and on the basic Christian communities in the Third World.

Basic Christian Communities

The story of the church in Mexico, Central America, and much of Latin America is largely the story of the suffering and oppression of the native peoples of those lands.[1] Catholicism came to that part of the world with the Spanish *conquistadores* and their Portuguese counterparts. These adventurers subdued the native populations, often at terrible cost, for their European monarchs. Millions of Aztecs and other native peoples died of disease in the years following the conquest of Mexico by Hernando Cortez in 1521. The remaining population was subjugated by the conquerors. Intermarriage between the Spaniards and the Indians produced a new culture and a new ruling elite in Mexico. But the vast majority of the population was made up of the poor and powerless native peoples. The story in Central America, Peru, Bolivia, Brazil, and parts of Argentina, Equador, and Colombia is similar.

Conquered and humiliated, the people of these countries recognized in the figure of the patient and long-suffering Savior the mirror image of their own suffering. The passion of Jesus has always been at the center of the popular piety of Latin American Catholicism as well as that of other countries which trace their religious and cultural roots to Spain. That piety finds expression in the tortured and bloody crucifixes found in so many Latin American churches or in the graphic reenactments of the way of the cross and crucifixion one finds in countries like Guatemala and the Philippines.

There was comfort to be found in the image of the patient, suffering Savior. But too often this image reinforced a passivity on the part of the people; what developed was a culture of poverty and dependence which kept the poor submissive, unable to take responsibility for their own lives. The Gospel had been emptied of its liberating power.

Unfortunately, the church which came with the conquerors too often did little to challenge the exploitation that accompanied the colonial system. There were exceptions, including a significant challenge to the exploitation of the native peoples. Dominican Bartolomé de Las Casas and a group of Spanish bishops led a struggle on behalf of the Indians during the period of 1544 to 1568.[2] Bishop Antonio de Valdivieso was murdered in Nicaragua in 1550 for speaking out on behalf of the Indians. The Jesuits attempted to develop communities free of colonial control for the Indians of Paraguay, Brazil, Argentina, and Bolivia in the seventeenth century; these "reductions" were very successful, but did not survive the expulsion of the Jesuits in 1767. There have been other exceptions. But all too often the church was either on the side of the ruling colonial power or fighting the emerging secular governments for its own rights and privileges.

But by the middle of the twentieth century the church in Latin America had begun entering a new chapter in its history. The years since the end of the Second World War have been marked by an increase in suffering for the peoples of many countries in Latin and Central America. All too often they have been the victims of repression and violence under military governments, usually supported by the United States.[3]

In Guatemala alone, over 100,000 civilians have been killed since the military took over in 1954, more than half of them in the last ten years. Most of them were killed by soldiers or by right wing death squads. Over twelve priests and three Protestant ministers have been murdered or disappeared. In El Salvador the Archbishop of San Salvador, Oscar Romero, was assassinated in 1980 while celebrating the Eucharist. At least seventeen priests have been murdered in El Salvador, including six Jesuits murdered together when armed and uniformed men entered their residence in November 1989. Throughout Central and Latin America, the number of lay leaders killed is in the thousands. These figures are not complete; it is difficult to calculate the number of those who have disappeared or been killed. But they indicate that at considerable cost, the church has begun to take the side of the people.

The first general conference of the Latin American Episcopal Conference (CELAM) at Rio de Janeiro in 1955 marked the beginning of a renewal. But the Second Vatican Council was the decisive influence. The Council was to affect Latin American Catholicism in a number of ways which were to have a lasting impact. It is difficult to overestimate the importance of the Decree on the Church in the Modern World (*Gaudium et Spes*), with its careful treatment of the responsibilities of the church in regard to issues of economic justice, human rights, development, and peace. The decree stressed that great efforts had to be made to satisfy the demands of justice and equity and it called Christians to a new level of concern for the poor.

The Decree on the Pastoral Office of Bishops in the Church (*Christus Dominus*) strongly recommended the establishment of national and regional episcopal conferences (CD 38). The bishops of Latin America returned to their churches determined to make greater use of their own episcopal conference. Their meetings at Medellín (1968) and Puebla (1979) sought to bring the renewal begun by the Council to their own churches. At Medellín and Puebla the bishops also endorsed to a considerable extent the themes of a new and uniquely Latin American theology, the theology of liberation. At Puebla they officially committed their churches to a preferential option for the poor. Most of all, at both conferences the bishops supported another post-conciliar movement with enormous potential for transforming the Latin American Church, the movement of basic Christian communities.

Base Communities

Called *comunidades eclesiales* or *comunidades eclesiais de base* (CEBs) in Latin America, these Basic Ecclesial Christian Communities (BECs) or Basic Christian Communities (BCCs) are often represented as a new way of being church.[4] In one sense this is true, as the BCCs are small communities of poor Christians who gather regularly for prayer and reflection on the Bible, fellowship, and action on behalf of the community. Almost always, their members come from the lower socio-economic levels of society, from the "base" or grassroots.

At the same time, the phenomenon of small groups of Christians gathering in community to live out the Gospel in a more radical way is nothing new in the history of the church.

Thus the BCCs are very much in the tradition of radical Christian communities throughout Christian history.

A BCC is generally formed when a group of people, most often neighbors, begin meeting one night a week to share their concerns and to reflect on them prayerfully in light of their faith. As the participants listen to each other's stories and join in singing the scripture-based songs of struggle and hope which have emerged from the BCCs, they become acquainted with each other on a new and deeper level. But it is the Bible that holds pride of place at the center of each meeting.

Until the Second Vatican Council the Roman Catholic Church did not encourage lay Catholics to read the Bible. Lessons from the Scripture were read of course in the liturgy, but Catholic preaching rarely involved a careful reflection on the biblical texts. Catholic parishioners heard sermons, not biblical homilies. In the U.S. prior to the Council children in Catholic schools read biblical stories in specially prepared texts, but not the Bible itself. Behind this reticence to place the Bible into the hands of the faithful was the fear of what was considered the Protestant penchant for "private interpretation." As a result, millions of Catholics grew up not really knowing very much about the Bible.

The Council, by endorsing and promoting the biblical and liturgical renewals already taking place in the church, ended this benign neglect of the Bible. Both the Dogmatic Constitution on Divine Revelation (*Dei Verbum*) and the Constitution on the Sacred Liturgy (*Sacrosanctum Concilium*) sought to give Scripture a new emphasis in the life and worship of the church. In mandating the revision of the liturgical texts, the Council sought to make the riches of Scripture more accessible to the people and it placed a new emphasis on preaching (SC 50-53). Priests, deacons, and catechists were told to share the word of God with those entrusted to them, while the faithful were encouraged to read the Bible frequently and to use it in their prayer (DV 25).

The result of the biblical renewal was an amazing rediscovery of the power of God's word. Rosemary Ruether has described the impact that this rediscovery of the word had on many Catholics who began to approach it as though for the first time.

They read the Bible much as medieval and Reformation radicals read it, as a critical and subversive document. They find in it a God who sides with the poor and with others despised by society; who, at the same time, confronts the social and religious institutions that are the tools of injustice.[5]

This is largely what happened when Latin American Christians, encouraged by their bishops at Medellín, began reading the Bible in small groups. They approached it, not to study and analyze it like the exegetes and theologians, but in order to allow it to illumine their own experience and give hope to their lives. They would ask each other: what is the living word of God saying to us today in the context of this community? Then they would share their interpretations with one another.

In the liturgy, priests familiar with liberation theology would often invite members of the congregation to offer their own insights during the homily. As they did so, they began to discover the prophetic condemnations of injustice, the good news Jesus addressed to the poor in his parables, the promise contained in his beatitudes. In this process, the poor themselves often become evangelists.[6]

Action for Justice

Julio de Santa Ana has worked for years in Sao Paulo, Brazil, a city which in fifteen years has swollen from a population of less than 3,000,000 to one of more than 14,000,000; she describes a typical meeting of a BCC. The meeting begins with prayer and song, a celebration of a common faith. Next the members spend some time talking about their common problems, seeking insight and understanding. Then they read and discuss the Scripture passage provided for the day. How does the word of God illumine their situation? Finally they seek consensus in regard to what needs to be done.[7]

If the BCCs confined themselves to biblical reflection, prayer, and community, they would not differ from other renewal movements, oriented towards the spiritual life of their members. But action for justice in response to the word of God is intrinsic to the BCCs. In Latin America many BCCs began when the poor in the crowded cities, particularly women, came together to pray. Their ability to address the experience of poverty, oppression, and powerlessness of so many impoverished peoples is the source of their potential for radical social transformation. The concrete needs of the members of individual BCCs remains their focus. From their sharing of concerns and biblical reflection their members begin to see more clearly the nature of their common problems. Thus, prayer and politics are often joined.

A Church from the Roots

The BCCs represent not so much a church *for* the poor as a church *of* the poor. They are essentially communities of lay people. Some are small groupings of families, generally of between 15 and 20 people. Others are considerably larger, and function as mini-parishes. A large parish may have a number of BCCs. Some BCCs are run by elected councils. Priests and sisters, "pastoral agents" working with BCCs, have helped keep them closely tied to the local church and, especially, to the local pastor. BCCs with active pastoral agents seem to be better organized and more active politically than those without them.[8] Many priests have learned a new, more personal and collaborative style of ministry through their work with the BCCs.

But the BCCs have also generated their own leaders "from the base." These "coordinators" often exercise a role of pastoral leadership which is called forth from the community rather than placed over it. They lead the prayer services, preach, minister to the sick, prepare individuals for baptism and confirmation, sometimes witness marriages. Thus the BCCs have already shown the possibility of an active church life without priests.

But without ordained ministers, the communities are not able to celebrate the Eucharist. Given the shortage of ordained ministers, theologians such as Leonardo Boff have raised the question as to the possibility of authorizing the lay coordinators to preside at the Eucharist in their communities.[9]

It is difficult to estimate just how many BCCs exist. The majority are in Brazil, where estimates run from 50,000 to almost 100,000. But they are to be found through much of Latin and Central America, as well as Mexico and the Philippines. Not all have accepted the movement towards basic Christian communities. Repressive governments frequently label BCCs as communist inspired and subversive. In many Third World countries, among them El Salvador, Honduras, Guatemala, and the Philippines, BCC organizers and leaders have been murdered.[10] Some members of the hierarchy have resisted the movement, fearing the more radical aspects of liberation theology and the danger of schism.

Sometimes the poor themselves resist this new idea of church, with the demands it makes upon them. They are often more comfortable with the traditional concept of the church they grew up with. One sister in Bolivia described this concept to me as a "church as spiritual gas station," where people come to be serviced, to buy their sacraments and their Masses for the dead. The poor are not used to expressing themselves in front of others, or of looking on priests and nuns as brothers and sisters, rather than as authority figures. But if some resist it, many more people have been empowered by the basic Christian community movement. It has already done much to revitalize the church in a considerable number of Third World countries.

Covenant Communities

In the Spring of 1967 a number of Catholic papers in the United States began carrying reports that some Catholic university professors and students at Duquesne University in Pittsburgh had undergone a pentecostal experience which included the gifts of tongues. They had received an outpouring or "baptism" of the Spirit while on a weekend retreat at the university. This "Duquesne weekend" was the beginning of the Catholic Charismatic Renewal Movement which was to become one of the major Catholic movements of the seventies.

What had led these rather traditional Roman Catholics, academics and students, like most of their coreligionists not very open to more demonstrative and affective expressions of religious feeling, to break out in tongues, tears, and cries of "praise the Lord"? To answer this it is necessary to go back to Duquesne in the autumn of 1966, when several lay faculty members began meeting to discuss and pray over their lives as Christians. They had read several books describing the pentecostal experience, among them David Wilkerson's *The Cross and the Switchblade*, and were attracted by the accounts of the Spirit's power working among those in the pentecostal movement.[11]

They sought help from various friends, among them an Episcopal priest and then a Presbyterian lay woman. In January 1967 they began attending the woman's prayer group. At the second meeting two of them asked the others to pray over them for the baptism in the Holy Spirit. Almost immediately Ralph Keifer, an instructor in theology, began to pray in tongues. The following week two more received the baptism in the Holy Spirit, perhaps best understood as personal experience of the Spirit's indwelling presence. In February the "Duquesne weekend" took place, when faculty members accompanied a group of about thirty students on a retreat.

From a small group at Duquesne, the movement spread like wildfire, or from a charismatic perspective, like the fires of Pentecost. In February Ralph Keifer, before his own baptism in the Spirit, had told some friends in South Bend, Indiana, about his newly awakened interest in pentecostalism. Among these friends were Kevin and Dorothy Ranaghan, both initially skeptical.[12] On March 5, shortly after Kiefer telephoned them about the Duquesne weekend, the Ranaghans met with a group from the University of Notre Dame for prayer, and felt themselves baptized in the Spirit. A week later they met in prayer with a group from the pentecostal Full Gospel Businessmen's Fellowship, and a number of them received the gift of tongues.

Some weeks later the Notre Dame group joined with a student group at Michigan State University, East Lansing, with similar results. Finally, a group of these Catholic pentecostals, by now attracting attention in the media, began holding weekly prayer meetings at Notre Dame. Some three thousand people came to the university for the summer session. Many of the nuns, priests, brothers, and lay religious educators attending became involved in the renewal, and then brought it back to their own churches and communities with them.

In the years that followed, charismatic communities sprung up across the country. Most of them were centered on the weekly prayer group meeting, usually a two or three hour meeting with various manifestations of the charismatic gifts. There would be readings from Scripture, prophecies and testimonies, praying and singing in tongues, lengthy teachings, and prayers with the laying on of hands for healing or the baptism in the Spirit. During the week small groups would meet for prayer and personal reflection on Scripture. Leaders in the group conducted Life in the Spirit seminars for those interested in the renewal.

Covenant Communities in the U.S.

In the seventies some of the larger charismatic communities began organizing themselves as "covenant communities." Basing themselves on Acts 2: 42-47, covenant communities are groups of Christians who publicly commit themselves to one another; they enter into a covenant to share their lives, their faith, and usually their resources. Organizationally, they are subdivided into households, each under a "head." A household may consist of a family, a group of single people, or others committed to celibacy, living as a "brotherhood" or "sisterhood." Most households meet daily for a period of common prayer.

In many ways the model has been the Word of God community in Ann Arbor, Michigan.[13] Ann Arbor's community was one of the first in the renewal; it began in November of 1967 at St. Mary's, a parish near the University of Michigan. Among its leaders were Steve Clark, Ralph Martin, and Gerry Rauch. The community grew rapidly in the early days. Within a few years the Thursday night prayer meeting was drawing groups of 400 to 500 people. A core community of those most deeply committed to the movement and to each other emerged in 1969; they began praying together as a community on Mondays. Various sub-communities, often of people living near each other, began to develop. As they prayed together they began to sense a call to covenant together.

In the summer of 1970 a number of groups committed themselves to live together in "households" or living groups. Each group took on a particular work or ministry and organized itself under a head, a male member responsible for coordinating the practical and spiritual life of the community. By the mid-seventies the Word of God Community had over a thousand adult members; by 1987 the number had grown to over 1500. It is 66 percent Roman Catholic, and has members from over fifteen other traditions. Within the community are four separate fellowships, Catholic, Free Church, Lutheran, and Reformed, which gather the members of a particular tradition together in relation to their church or confessional family.

Other covenant communities began emerging out of prayer communities. For their members they provided a supportive environment for living an explicit Christian life. Shared prayer and worship were at the center. Many took part in the Eucharist on a daily basis, and prayed morning prayer and evening prayer from the office. Members of a household would meet weekly to deal with personal problems and to share their religious experience. Many families became involved. Others lived in households for singles or in the special households for those committed to celibacy. Sharing their incomes bound them together financially and made their mutual dependence real. They took on various ministries and apostolic works. One community in Georgia made a commitment to live with low income poor families in a public housing complex.

The Conference on Charismatic Renewal in the Christian Churches, held in 1977 in Kansas City, Missouri, was probably the high water mark of the movement in the United States. The Conference was ecumenical, involving Charismatic Catholics and mainline Protestants as well as classical pentecostals, both black and white. Some 45,000 people took part, half of them Catholic. Cardinal Suenens of Belgium addressed the group, as well as Ruth Carter Stapleton, a Southern Baptist and sister of Jimmy Carter, elected president of the U.S. a year earlier. But attendance at the subsequent national Catholic conferences at Notre Dame decreased considerably.

After the Kansas City Conference a split in the Catholic charismatic movement became more evident. Two different directions had been present in the renewal. The two communities which had assumed the leadership of the renewal on the national level, Word of God at Ann Arbor and People of Praise at South Bend, had long emphasized covenant communities over parish-oriented Catholic prayer groups. This part of the renewal movement, represented by the magazine, *New Covenant*, has been described as "the trend towards tightly organized, hierarchical communities, theological conservatism, and lessened attention to the Catholic tradition."[14] Other renewal communities were more parish-oriented. A new magazine, the *Catholic Charismatic*, appeared in 1976 to represent this direction.

After the Kansas City Conference, some covenant communities such as the City of the Angels in Los Angeles declared themselves to be ecumenical, even though the vast majority of their members were Catholics. This meant that the Eucharist was no longer a part of the weekly prayer meeting. Though their members continued to attend their respective churches, there was no longer a sacramental dimension to the prayer meeting.

The ecumenical direction also had the effect of distancing the covenant communities somewhat from the authority of the hierarchy. Any tensions which may have existed between the covenant communities and the rest of the Catholic charismatic renewal diminished in the 1980s, partly because of a more inclusive emphasis in *New Covenant* and partly as a result of the formation of the Bishops Liaison Committee with Catholic Charismatic Renewal.

As of 1987, some 7,600 adults are in communities associated through a network with Word of God and another 3,000 people, including children, are in communities associated with People of Praise. Other covenant communities in the United States include Mother of God in Gaithersburg, Maryland and Lamb of God in Baltimore; People of Hope in Newark, New Jersey; People of Praise at South Bend; Alleluja in Augusta, Georgia; Community of God's Delight in Dallas, Texas; and City of the Lord in Phoenix, Arizona (resulting from the 1981 merger of City of the Angels in Los Angeles and People of Joy in Phoenix).

New Communities in France

The charismatic renewal in France developed as part of a more general spiritual renewal which was to lead to an extraordinary flowering of new communities, both charismatic and monastic.[15] The first charismatic prayer groups appeared in France in the early seventies. Within a few years a number of charismatic communities appeared, related in various ways to the charismatic renewal. Monique Hébrard has studied twelve of them: *Théophanie, Chemin Neuf, Emmanuel, Lion de Juda et L'Agneau Immolé, Fondation, Pain de vie, Berdine, Puits de Jacob, Réjouis-toi, "Source" de Lens, Siloé*, and *Sainte-Croix* which was dissolved in 1984.[16]

Most of these are covenant communities. Some, such as *Emmanuel* (1972) and *Chemin Neuf* (1973), are urban communities which consist of a core group of full members who live together, and a far larger group of associates who gather regularly for prayer, preaching, and evangelization. *Chemin Neuf* has some 2,000 full and associate members, *Emmanuel* has 3,500. In 1987 more than 20,000 people, most of them young, took part in various assemblies sponsored by *Emmanuel*. Others, such as *Théophanie*, (1972) *Lion de Juda* (1975), and *Pain de Vie* (1976) are semimonastic. They as well as *Emmanuel* are mixed communities of families, priests and those preparing for ordination, and others consecrated to celibacy.

Of all the French covenant communities, *Lion de Juda* is the most oriented towards the contemplative life. Its founder, Gérard Croissant, was a Protestant pastor who became a Catholic and took the name Ephraim. He is a deacon, the husband of Jo, and has a daughter. The members of *Lion de Juda* consider themselves as living a new form of the monastic life which brings together in community married couples and their children and men and women consecrated to celibacy. They gather regularly for the office which includes singing in tongues. As their name suggests, the community has a special concern for the Jewish people, praying for their integration into the Body of Christ, celebrating on Friday the Shabbat service, often chanting some of the psalms in Hebrew. The community has some 400 adult members and thirteen houses in France.

The French communities differ from their American counterparts in a number of ways. First, they are far more diverse. Second, they are more closely linked to the official church. Many of those in France have been recognized in various dioceses by the bishops and have been given pastoral responsibilities. Some such as *Chemin Neuf, Emmanuel, Lion de Juda,* and *Pain de Vie* have a canonical status as associations of the faithful. New members make their commitment before the group, as in a religious order. Third, they are more liturgically oriented, with an emphasis on praying the office and adoration of the Blessed Sacrament.[17] Communities such as *Lion de Juda* and *Pain de Vie* practice perpetual adoration; their members take turns praying before the sacrament day and night. Those committing themselves to celibacy within the various communities have become in effect members of alternative religious communities; in communities like *Lion de Juda* and *Emmanuel* they wear a religious habit.

These communities have been a strong force for evangelization in France and have made considerable efforts to reach out to the poor and the marginalized. *Chemin Neuf* carries out ministries of spiritual formation, religious education, and various services to the disadvantaged. *Pain de Vie* welcomes and works with prostitutes, recently released prisoners, and those with drug problems. *Lion de Juda* has a ministry for the sick which includes both medical and psychological assistance and prayers for healing. The community also sponsors an association to aid women considering abortion. These two communities as well as *Emmanuel* work with people who have AIDS. There are probably some 10,000 involved in the new communities in France, while more than 100,000 are touched in various ways by their ministries. It is said that three-fourths of the recent vocations to the priesthood in France come from the charismatic renewal.

Conclusion

While there have been some attempts to identify covenant communities with the basic Christian communities of the Third World,[18] it generally remains true that covenant communities represent a middle class movement, while the BCCs are communities of the poor. There are some notable exceptions. The members of *Pain de Vie* in France live an extreme poverty. But in poor countries like Mexico, there has been considerable conflict between the BCC movement and the charismatic renewal.[19]

BCCs, far more concerned with the transformation of society, involve not just communal prayer but also social engagement and political action. The renewal communities tend to be focused much more on personal piety, spiritual development, and particularly in France, evangelization.

An insufficient concern for social justice has long been one criticism of the charismatic renewal and covenant communities. An overemphasis on healings, divine interventions, and miracles can easily distract believers from the challenge of facing everyday social issues. But there are other criticisms. Some have found these communities too inward looking, concerned more for their own spiritual development than for the renewal of the greater church.

In developing its own hierarchical leadership, the trend in the renewal represented by the covenant communities in some ways has replicated the development of authority in the history of the church. The doctrine of male "headship" and female "submission" in these communities has drawn considerable criticism. In 1971 Josephine Massyngberde Ford, a theology professor at Notre Dame who was involved in the renewal in the early days at South Bend, argued that the Ann Arbor—South Bend neo-pentecostalism had unconsciously adopted a theology similar to that of the Radical Reformation. Specifically she challenged its rigid hierarchy, its way of teaching, its subordination of women, and its sectarian withdrawal from the world.[20]

What is the future of these movement communities? In the United States the charismatic renewal peaked at the end of the seventies. The number and membership of covenant communities today seems to be decreasing or at least remaining stable, though the movement in France is still quite strong and has considerable support from the hierarchy.

There is also some question as to the continued growth of the BCC movement in Latin America. In his study W.E.

Hewitt notes that the Brazilian church seems to be placing more emphasis today on popular movements in the secular sphere such as trade unions and political parties, rather than promoting the BCCs as the instruments of social change. The advancing of more conservative bishops to the hierarchy in Latin America may also be a factor.[21]

There also seems to be a rather high turnover of members in the BCCs. Research on BCCs in the archdiocese of Sao Paulo in Brazil indicates that in the oldest BCCs, from 10 to 17 years in age, no members have been affiliated with a community for more than seven years.[22]

But whatever their future, these communities have already played an important role in the church. The charismatic renewal and the covenant communities to which it gave rise have helped many Roman Catholics to develop a more loving image of God and to become comfortable with a more spontaneous and affective style of prayer. Many Catholics have become reconnected with the church through the renewal and have moved on to deeper levels of prayer and engagement.

The covenant communities have placed considerable emphasis on ecumenism. They have helped many Catholics and mainline Protestants to discover the extent to which they share a common faith with each other and with pentecostal Christians, and thus have been an impetus toward Christian unity. For the French communities especially, ecumenism always includes the Jewish people, not so much to convert them to a particular church but to enable them to recognize Jesus as the messiah. This would involve the kind of conversion called for by the prophets. These communities also place considerable emphasis on Jerusalem as a center for Christian unity and the place for the revelation of the second coming of Christ.

The BCC movement has awakened a biblically based popular religiosity in Third World countries and brought hundreds of thousands of Christians to a new and vital involvement in the life of the church. The BCCs have developed a new group of effective pastoral leaders from the grass roots. Most of all, they have empowered the poor, both within the church and within their often oppressive societies. Challenging the passivity which is the inheritance of a culture of poverty and dependence, they have enabled the poor to take on a new responsibility for their own lives.

Both basic Christian communities and covenant communities have helped many to find in Scripture a powerful source for prayer and personal guidance and thus to come to a more personal and vital relationship with God. The two movements have been important forces for renewal and exemplify a rediscovery by lay Christians of the communal nature of the Christian life.

10.

Radical Christian Communities: Signs of the Kingdom

In our study we have seen that the impulse towards radical Christian community has been coextensive with Christian history. In every period of the church men and women have sought to live out the Gospel call to radical discipleship in community with one another.

Though this impulse produced religious orders throughout history, and continues to lead to the establishment of new religious communities, we have also seen that many of these movements were originally movements of lay people. The monastic movement itself in its early history was largely a movement of lay people who left the cities and towns in order to live a more radical Christian discipleship in the wilderness.

The evangelical awakening which swept through Europe in the twelfth and thirteenth centuries sought to establish radical Christian communities in its towns and cities. It too was a movement which had a decidedly lay character to it. The Humiliati, the Waldensians, and the Poor Catholics represented mixed communities of lay men and women who sought to live a Gospel life modeled on the poverty of the apostles. The Beguines and the Beghards were lay movements. The Franciscans, lay in inspiration, became increasingly clerical as they became established.

For centuries, communities of women had to accept a monasticization of their life in order to gain church approval. The "lesser sisters" who gathered around Clare of Assisi sought to live a life similar to the "lesser brothers" of Francis, but with the imposition of convents and cloister they became a cloistered contemplative order. From Clare's time down to the middle of the nineteenth century, communities of women dedicated to ministry were required to adopt cloister and monastic practices.

But there has been a positive side as well to the church's efforts at regulating religious communities. Ecclesial recognition brought many communities the guidance which kept them in communion with the church. The story of the Waldensians, who moved from a critical attitude towards abuses in the church, particularly on the part of the clergy, to a rejection of church teachings, is tragic but still instructive. And it is not the only such story. The twelfth and thirteenth centuries provide numerous examples of movements which began as reforms and ended in schism and doctrinal heterodoxy.

Recognition by the church, with the institutionalization that implied, also gave many communities the stability which enabled them to survive. They received rules, privileges, patrons, and canonical status. Thus some Christian communities became in time religious orders and congregations. They have played an important role in the church's history, providing many talented and dedicated men and women for its service. Furthermore, by offering a continuing witness to the ideal of communal life based on the Gospel, they have helped keep the vision of radical Christian community alive.

One negative effect of this institutionalization of religious life was that it removed the opportunity for other Christians not considered canonically as "religious" to live lives of radical discipleship in community.

The radical wing of the sixteenth century Reformation, in its efforts to restore what it understood to be the apostolic church of primitive Christianity, in a sense sought to provide that lost opportunity for lay Christians to live the radical Gospel. As Mel Piehl has pointed out, with the Reformation the advocacy of radical Gospel ideas past almost entirely to Protestantism.[1]

The Moravians, the Hutterites, the Mennonites, and the Quakers all represented alternative Christian communities which distanced themselves from their surrounding societies. They same thing could be said for the Shaker and Oneida movements in early nineteenth century America. However marginal they might be within Protestantism, they were communities which took a countercultural stance even if they did not always go so far as to challenge the prevailing social order in the name of the Gospel.

Religious life not only survived the upheaval of the sixteenth century, but continued on renewed, revitalized by reformers like Teresa of Avila and by new communities such as the Jesuits and an increasing number of women's communities committed to service.

Contemporary Christian Communities

The twentieth century has brought its own challenges to radical Christian communities. But in its final decades, they continue to be much in evidence. Traditional religious communities have experienced profound changes as a result of the renewal begun by the Second Vatican Council and the social and cultural changes which coincided with it. New religious communities have been established.

A number of lay communities have appeared, many of them formed to carry out a Gospel ministry to the disadvantaged. Covenant communities have emerged from the charismatic renewal and basic Christian communities have been formed, particularly but not exclusively in Third World countries. Each community, lay or religious, can be described as radical in so far as it represents a community of Christians who chose to live a life based on the Gospel which stands at some critical distance from its surrounding culture.

Thus the twentieth century has witnessed a number of powerful currents which have challenged but also nurtured and reinvigorated the impulse towards radical Christian community.

Contemplation and Solidarity with the Poor

One of the most powerful of these currents has been the combination of a contemplative spirituality with a commitment to solidarity with the poor. In many ways Charles de Foucauld can be regarded as the modern exemplar of this way of life, though it remained for the Little Sisters and Little Brothers who came after him to first live out his open monasticism and model it for others. Mother Teresa is another example of this charism. And there are numerous contemporary communities, both lay and religious, which have sought a similar life of discipleship combining prayer, simplicity of life, and the direct service of the poor.

For the Little Brothers and Little Sisters of Jesus and the Missionaries of Charity, eucharistic adoration provides a focus for their contemplative spirituality. The same is true for covenant communities such as *Lion de Juda* and *Pain de Vie*, for the l'Arche community at Trosly-Breuil, and for many of the l'Arche communities worldwide.

Contemporary Monasticism

A second current, often flowing together with the first, has been a rediscovery of monasticism in the Protestant tradition. Grandchamp, Pomeyrol, and the Marienschwestern of Darmstadt are contemporary Protestant communities living a monastic life. Taizé has become an ecumenical monastic community. The vitality and influence of these communities testifies to the enduring value of the monastic life in the church. Within the Catholic tradition, monastic life has continued to flourish and has been enriched by the establishment of a number of new communities such as the Monastic Family of Bethlehem.

The Struggle for Justice

A third current moves beyond prayer and direct service of the poor to challenge the contemporary social order in the name of the Gospel. Communities like the Catholic Worker, Iona, and Sojourners are prophetic communities actively involved in the struggle for justice. Their members live out a discipleship which seeks not only to minister to the hungry and the persecuted, but also to bring about the change of institutions and structures responsible for their condition.

Many contemporary religious communities have become deeply involved in the struggle for justice; some of their members have paid the ultimate price with their lives. The same is

true for many members of the basic Christian communities in
Latin America and the Philippines. The basic Christian community movement in Third World countries can be understood
as part of a twentieth century phenomenon which has been
described as the "irruption of the poor into history."

Christian community is not limited to those communities
we have described as radical; it can be present in ordinary
parishes and congregations, in schools, and in the home. But
these radical communities are successful today and are valued
even by those not drawn to live in them because they meet a
number of contemporary needs.

First, they meet the need felt by many people for a deeper
spirituality. In a secular age, many are searching for some
experience of the sacred. They often find that the worship of
their churches lacks any sense of the holy; their liturgies and
services are too often overly verbal, trite, and carried out with
little reverence. Radical Christian communities proclaim the
primacy of the sacred. Prayer and worship are always central.

They also reveal the sacred by their way of life, not by
withdrawing from the world but by the way they chose to be
present within it. Their simple and detached lifestyle says that
material possessions are always secondary. Work has an
important place in the lives of their members, and is done with
a remarkable single-mindedness. Even little jobs are done well.
But work is done to meet practical needs or offered as a
service; it is not a means to advancement. People are more
important than things.

Because the environment is part of nature and reflects the
hand of its creator, it is treated with respect. Thus many Christian communities have an instinctive sense for the ecology. A
sense of order and proportion, part of the legacy of monasticism, often characterizes the places where they live. Some
flowers, a piece of wood, a woven wall hanging, a candle set
before a picture; the simplest things, arranged with care, can
point beyond the immediate to the hidden beauty of God.

Second, Christian communities offer a way of structuring
life for those who experience a call to service and simplicity in
the name of the Gospel. As alternative, countercultural communities they are attractive to many disaffected with a self-
centered and materialistic society.

Third, they are able to model a vision of community in an often fragmented society. Many people today long for a communal life which transcends natural relationships. The example of men and women, single and married, able to live in communities of friends and companions, sustained by their faith, is a sign of hope.

Finally, Christian communities continue to illustrate the value of celibacy "for the sake of the kingdom." This is particularly true of religious communities. Whatever might be said about its religious or mystical meaning, celibacy makes possible a total commitment to a way of life. Many communities have found it difficult to keep married couples involved in the life of the community. For couples, each must be totally committed. A commitment to a community cannot be sustained if does not involve both partners.

Challenges for the Future

What are some of the challenges faced by radical Christian communities today?

1. Remaining Countercultural

First, maintaining the radical character of communities which exist to enable their members to live out the Gospel in a radical way is a particular challenge. In a secularized culture, these communities should be countercultural communities; they are not ends in themselves but exist for a particular calling or ministry. This means a commitment to a simple lifestyle, prayer, and a continual reflection on the Gospel.

But there is always the temptation to make accommodations, to decrease the distance between the community and its surrounding culture, to mitigate the demands of the original vision. When this happens, a community ceases to be radical. No longer a means for living out a particular vision of the Gospel, it becomes simply a comfortable home for its members.

Because Christian communities generally offer congenial and supportive environments, there is a danger today of making the supportive community an end in itself rather than a means to a life of discipleship, especially when those drawn to a community come with unfulfilled needs and unrealistic expectations.

Many communities today find this a problem, with so many coming from broken families, damaged relationships, and unhappy backgrounds. Often the possibility of living in a non-threatening and accepting environment is a major factor in drawing them to a community. Though a genuine Christian community should be able to facilitate the growth of its members, an apostolic community is not a therapeutic community. To expect it to function as one is to frustrate its true purpose. The same thing is true for monastic communities.

At the same time, the importance of the community's calling or ministry should not blind its members to the relationships which will sustain them in carrying it out. A community needs to devote time to the growth and formation of its members. Relationships in the community are particularly important and take time to develop. Married couples need time and space for themselves.

Living a healthy celibate life is another challenge. A commitment to celibacy helps sustains a community, but it also needs to be sustained by a community. A community's way of life should enable its members to continue to mature as responsible individuals and at the same time to grow in their capacities for friendship and intimacy. A community which encourages a juvenile dependency in its members, whether on authority, or in their relationships, or in the irresponsible use of the community's goods, is not a healthy one.

Jim Wallis, one of the founding members of Sojourners, has commented on the need to unite the prophetic and pastoral imperatives of biblical faith in the life of a Christian community. A community formed around a common vision needs to find a pastoral way to nurture that vision in the life of its members; without this pastoral care, the vision itself can become an oppressive and destructive burden. But at the same time, "without a prophetic voice challenging God's people to lay their lives down for justice in the world, pastoral nurture and ministry can easily degenerate into a self-serving group welfare, or an unbiblical inward preoccupation."[2] A healthy community needs to both challenge and support its members.

2. *Tension Between Spirit and Structure*

There is an inevitable tension between spirit and structure in the life of radical Christian communities. A community usually develops out of a movement or around a charismatic individual whose vision and personality draws others to join him or her in living out some particular vision of the Gospel. But if a community is to survive the period of its origin, it must develop ways to institutionalize its original vision and its own life of discipleship.

The church has been involved in this process of institutionalization by reviewing and granting canonical recognition to community rules of life and by exercising a pastoral care for those who live by them. This effort on the part of the church to guide and regulate religious communities has given them stability and kept them in the church's communion, as we saw earlier.

But with institutionalization comes also the danger of comlacency and stagnation. Often some of the original vitality is lost, and the spirit can easily be stifled. There always remains the challenge of reconciling spirit and structure, charism and institution, personal liberty and the demands of communal life.

Contemporary communities such as l'Arche and Sojourners which developed in the midst of the anti-institutionalism of the 60s and 70s have come in the 80s to appreciate the importance of structure. Even Catholic Worker communities are not as unstructured as they sometimes appear to be. Without some kind of effective structure, a community cannot deal with the various crises which inevitably arise. For l'Arche communities, entering into community with handicapped people raised the question for the assistants of what would happen to the handicapped members if the assistants left the community. They have had to face the crucial issue of permanence and stability. The Sojourners community in its early days experimented with an implicit rather than explicit leadership. But ultimately the experiment failed because they found that implicit leaders cannot really be held accountable.

Vatican II did much to enable many Catholic religious communities to rediscover and reappropriate the vision of their founders, as we have seen. According to Sandra Schneiders, one positive sign of the health of contemporary religious life is that after several centuries of almost total institutionalization, the 'movement' character of religious life is reasserting itself.[3]

But there are still many challenges facing contemporary Christian communities which reflect the tension between spirit and structure. A serious problem for the Catholic Church is the alienation experienced by many dedicated women religious because of the church's exclusion of women from its ordained ministry and its decision-making structures. Some religious women must still struggle to exercise self-determination in their own religious congregations. Some communities of religious women have become non-canonical communities and others may move in that direction.

Another challenge comes from the increasingly ecumenical character of many contemporary Christian communities, including some religious ones. Many communities face the difficult and frequently painful question of trying to incorporate people from different Christian traditions into a worshipping community while continuing to respect and maintain their communion with their respective churches. It is difficult to support a genuine community life, with a common life of worship, while the churches remain divided.

3. *Attracting New Members*

Another challenge today for many communities, both religious and lay, is attracting new members who will make permanent commitments to the community and its life. Many communities experience a high turnover of those who do come to join them. Religious communities in particular are feeling the shortage of candidates.[4] Some communities of religious women have seen five or more years pass without a single novice. Some communities will disappear. Some will have to combine with other congregations that have similar spiritualities and works.

The life of many of these communities continues to be simple, often rigorous. They need to find creative ways of sharing their experience of Christian community with others who might be interested in their way of living out the Gospel and join them permanently.

For a time in the sixties, the Benedictine monastery of Niederaltaich in Germany ran an experiment called *Kloster auf Zeit* or temporary monasticism, offering young men the opportunity of spending periods of several weeks living in the monastery as monks. A number of American monasteries currently offer various programs allowing a temporary participation in the monastic life.[5] Perhaps other religious communities could find ways to institutionalize temporary commitments. In this way they could incorporate men and women drawn to share in their lives and ministries for an extended but limited period of time.

Another kind of temporary, countercultural community is represented by post-college service communities such as the Jesuit Volunteer Corps, the Jesuit International Volunteers, or the Claretian Volunteers. They generally involve a one or two year commitment, a simple lifestyle in an inner city community, and working with the disadvantaged as unpaid volunteers. Some communities such as the Los Angeles Catholic Worker offer summer internship programs. In Europe a considerable number of young people have been drawn to the monastic life after living for a time in communities such as l'Arche which have a strong emphasis on prayer.

4. *Ministry and Ordination*

Another challenge today, a new one, comes in the area of eucharistic presidency. The shortage of priests together with a new sense of the importance of lay ministry has increasingly raised the question of ordaining lay pastoral leaders to preside at the Eucharist in their communities. Many basic Christian communities in Third World countries are pastored by lay men and women who have been recognized by their communities as pastoral leaders. In Africa lay catechists often serve as pastors for local churches in the absence of ordained ministers. The lay leader of one French charismatic community, since dissolved, caused a stir by asking his bishop for ordination, and the idea has occurred to others.[6] Many of these communities want to at least have some say in the choice of their ordained ministers.

For many communities today the exclusion of women from the priesthood has been particularly painful. This is especially true for some communities of Catholic religious women. Because some of their members refuse to participate in eucharistic liturgies presided over by men, they find themselves divided precisely at the Lord's table which should be the center of their unity as a community.

A similar issue has surfaced in at least one Catholic Worker community. Casa Maria, the Catholic Worker community in Milwaukee, has invited women, laymen and sometimes non-Catholics to preside at its eucharistic liturgies.[7] But such unilateral action has been divisive within the community and jeopardizes the community's communion with the church.

Besides the question of ordaining community leaders, the question of acknowledging a preaching role for lay leaders who show a charism for preaching has surfaced again, as it did in the twelfth century.

The Catholic Church needs to find new ways to recognize that all are called to share in the church's mission and ministry without confusing the distinct roles of ordained and lay ministers. Can it find a way to provide for some lay preaching without devaluing the preaching mission entrusted to the ordained? Could the church authorize those who demonstrate a charism for pastoral and liturgical leadership to preside at the Eucharist in their communities and still maintain the church's communion? Will it be able to move beyond the present impasse over the question of women in ordained ministry? These are particularly vexing, yet challenging questions. They will continue to be raised by radical Christian communities within the church.

5. *The Call to Holiness*

Finally, communities modeled on the Gospel should be expected to call their members to holiness of life. This is not to suggest that those in Christian communities, lay or religious, have chosen a "higher state" or lead a life superior to that of other Christians. All Christians are called to holiness.

But communities which are truly or radically Christian

should be examples of holiness for the entire church. Those communities involved in the struggle for justice and the changing of unjust structures have a special need for the witness of contemplative and monastic communities, with their reminder that authentic Christian life must always be rooted in prayer and worship.

At the same time, justice communities remind others that genuine discipleship can never be disengaged from the world and the concerns of its peoples, that it is costly, and that it must embody concretely the values of the kingdom.

Conclusion

Traditionally, the religious life, with vows of poverty, chastity, and obedience, has been described as a sign of the kingdom. The Second Vatican Council reaffirmed this understanding,[8] and in his recent letter on Religious Life in the United States Pope John Paul II said that religious "offer a viable and feasible alternative to what is and speak the promise of what is to be."[9] But this symbolic function is not restricted to canonical or even non-canonical religious communities. Any Christian community whose members seek to live the Gospel in a radical way stands as a sign of the kingdom.

L'Arche communities welcome as valued members mentally handicapped men and women deeply hurt by the isolation and rejection they have so often experienced. The members of justice communities like the Catholic Worker and Sojourners seek to embody the beatitudes in their everyday lives; they live by values and make decisions which seem naive or impractical in the "real" world. The Missionaries of Charity dedicate themselves to "the poorest of the poor," and numerous other communities minister to those who fall through the cracks of our depersonalized, modern societies. Celibacy lived out generously for the sake of the kingdom continues to challenge others who cannot understand how such a life is possible. Monastic communities often communicate to their visitors a profound sense of peace. Their prayer reminds others of the nearness of God.

Brother Roger frequently speaks of Taizé as a "parable of community." That is to say, Taizé invites others to experience what the church itself should be. This is true of all Christian communities whose lives are radically rooted in the Gospel. They are signs of the compassionate service of the poor, reconciliation of people, holiness of life, and communion with Christ characteristic of the kingdom.

For many people today, these communities are the clearest signs of God's presence in our midst.

Monk reading, Monastic Family of Bethlehem

Notes, Introduction

[1] William L. Shirer, *The Nightmare Years 1930-1940* (Boston: Little, Brown and Company, 1984), pp. 149-55; William J. O'Malley points out that among the 2,579 Catholic priests, brothers, and seminarians imprisoned at Dachau were 447 German and Austrian priests; "The Priests of Dachau," *America* 157 (1987) pp. 351-52.

[2] Johann Baptist Metz, *The Emergent Church: The Future of Christianity in a Postbourgeois World* (New York: Crossroad, 1986), p. 27.

[3] Ibid., p. 1-2.

Notes, Chapter 1

[1] Edward Schillebeeckx, *Jesus: An Experiment in Christology* (New York: Seabury Press, 1979), p. 98.

[2] Ibid., p. 127.

[3] Ibid., p. 153.

[4] Albert Nolan, *Jesus before Christianity* (Maryknoll, NY: Orbis Books, 1978), p. 84.

[5] Ibid., p. 139.

[6] Jon Sobrino, *Christology at the Crossroads* (Maryknoll, NY: Orbis Books, 1978), pp. 57-58.

[7] Johann Baptist Metz, *The Emergent Church* (New York: Crossroad, 1986), pp. 14-15.

[8] Elisabeth Schüssler Fiorenza, *In Memory of Her* (New York: Crossroad, 1983), pp. 120-29.

[9] Ibid., p. 135.

[10] Sacred Congregation for the Doctrine of the Faith, *Instruction on Certain Aspects of the "Theology of Liberation"* (Boston: Daughters of St. Paul, 1984), p. 16.

[11] L. John Topel, *The Way to Peace: Liberation Through the Bible* (Maryknoll, NY: Orbis Books, 1976), p. 22.

[12] See for example Jan Lambrecht *The Sermon on the Mount* (Wilmington, DE: Michael Glazier, 1985), p. 40.

[13] See Raymond E. Brown, *The Birth of the Messiah* (Garden City, NY: Doubleday, 1979), pp. 350-55 on the Jewish-Christian *anawim*.

[14] Topel, *The Way to Peace*, p. 185, note 5.

[15] Leonardo Boff, *Jesus Christ Liberator* (Maryknoll, NY: Orbis Books, 1978), p. 76.

[16] In his study, *The Scholastic Analysis of Usury* (Cambridge, MA: Harvard

University Press, 1957), John T. Noonan indicates that the medieval teaching was based not simply on the New Testament, but on the Christian tradition which appealed to the writings of the fathers and various condemnations of clerical usurers by early councils, as well as to the Old Testament; p. 11.

[17]Schüssler Fiorenza, *In Memory of Her*, pp. 121-23.

[18]Hans Küng, *On Being a Christian* (Garden City, NY: Doubleday, 1976), p. 200.

[19]Andrew M. Greeley, "Empirical Liturgy: the Search for Grace," *America* 157 (1987), p. 379.

[20]See for example, Dietrich Bonhoeffer, *The Cost of Discipleship* (New York: Macmillan, 1963).

Notes, Chapter 2

[1]Thomas Merton, *The Seven Storey Mountain* (New York: Harcourt, Brace and Company, 1948), pp. 364-65.

[2]*Life of St. Anthony*, ch. 2, trans. Mary Emily Keenan, in *Early Christian Biographies*, ed. Roy J. Deferrari (Washington, D.C., 1952), pp. 135-36.

[3]See for example Herbert Workman, *The Evolution of the Monastic Ideal* (Boston: Beacon Press, 1962), pp. 7-14; Thomas M. Gannon and George W. Traub, *The Desert and the City* (London: Collier-Macmillan, 1969), pp. 21-25.

[4]See Jerome, *Life of Paul*, 6.

[5]The transition from a less institutionalized relationship of master and disciples to a more structured obedience to a superior did not happen either easily or at once. See Philip Rousseau, *Ascetics, Authority, and the Church* (Oxford University Press, 1978), pp. 49-55.

[6]See Rousseau, *Ascetics, Authority and the Church*, pp. 62-67.

[7]Gannon and Traub, *The Desert and the City*, p. 40.

[8]See Anne Yarborough, "Civilization in the Fourth Century: The Example of Roman Women," *Church History* 45 (1976) 157.

[9]Jerome, *Letters*, no. 61.

[10]Rousseau, *Ascetics, Authority and the Church*, pp. 81-95.

[11]Augustine, *Confessions* Book 8, chs. 6 ff.

[12]See John Ryan, *Irish Monasticism* (Dublin: Irish Academic Press, 1986 [first edition 1931]), pp. 59 ff.

[13]In addition to Ryan, *Irish Monasticism*, see Kathleen Hughes and Ann Hamlin, *Celtic Monasticism: The Modern Traveler to the Early Irish Church* (New York: Seabury, 1981), pp. 4-18.

[14]For a description of monastic buildings, see David Knowles, *Christian Monasticism* (New York: McGraw-Hill, 1969), pp. 98-107. Knowles argues that the cloister was probably derived from the court at the west end of Italian basilicas, rather than from the *atrium* of the large Roman house, p. 98.

[15]For the history of the office see Robert Taft, *The Liturgy of the Hours in East and West* (Collegeville, MN: The Liturgical Press, 1986).

[16]Ibid., p. 55.

[17]Ibid., pp. 66-67.

[18]See Henrietta Leyser, *Hermits and the New Monasticism* (New York: St. Martin's Press, 1984), p. 49; also Caroline Walker Bynum, *Jesus as Mother*, (Berkeley: University of California Press, 1982), p. 14.

[19]Leyser reports the rumor that Robert slept among his women disciples, "perhaps as the ultimate test of victory over his body"; *Hermits and the New Monasticism*, p. 50. Ghandi is said to have done the same.

[20]See especially Bynum, *Jesus as Mother*, pp. 62-66.

[21]Aelred of Rievaulx, *Spiritual Friendship*, trans. Mary Eugenia Laker, Cistercian Fathers Series No. 5 (Washington, D.C.: Cistercian Publications, 1974).

[22]Louis Bouyer, *The Cistercian Heritage* (Westminster, MD: Newman Press, 1958), p. 65.

[23]C.H. Lawrence, *Medieval Monasticism*, (London: Longman, 1984), p. 153.

[24]For a look at a number of contemporary monastic communities, see Walter Capps, *The Monastic Impulse* (New York: Crossroad, 1983); also Charles A. Fracchia, *Living Together Alone: The New American Monasticism* (San Francisco: Harper & Row, 1979).

[25]See especially Thomas Merton, *Contemplation in a World of Action* (Garden City, NY: Doubleday, 1973).

[26]See Michael Mott, *The Seven Mountains of Thomas Merton* (Boston: Houghton Mifflin Company, 1984), pp. 435-54.

[27]Thomas Merton, *Contemplation in a World of Action*, p. 242.

Notes, Chapter 3

[1]See Lester K. Little, *Religious Poverty and the Profit Economy in Medieval Europe* (Ithica, NY: Cornell University Press, 1978), pp. 35-41.

[2]C.H. Lawrence, *Medieval Monasticism* (London and New York: Longman, 1984), pp. 125-127.

[3]M.-D. Chenu, *Nature, Man, and Society in the Twelfth Century* (Chicago & London: University of Chicago Press, 1968), pp. 242-243.

[4]Leonardo Boff, *St. Francis: A Model for Human Liberation* (New York: Crossroad, 1985). p. 56.

[5]Ronald A. Knox, *Enthusiasm* (New York & Oxford: Oxford University Press, 1950), p. 71. Knox suggests that beneath the various medieval movements lie "two streams . . . of opposition to the medieval hierarchy," the Waldensians and the Cathars; p. 72.

[6]Lester K. Little, *Religious Poverty and the Profit Economy*, p. 143.

[7]Cf. Samuel Torvend, "Lay Spirituality in Medieval Christianity," *Spirituality Today* 35 (1983) 117-26.

[8]Chenu, *Nature, Man, and Society*, p. 260.

[9]See William A. Hinnebusch, *The History of the Dominican Order*, Vol. 1 (Staten Island, NY: Alba House, 1966), p. 24.

[10]*Walter Map's "De Nuqis Curalium,"* trans. Montague R. James (London: Cymmrodorion, 1923), p. 66.

[11]Ernest W. McDonnell, *The Beguines and Beghards in Medieval Culture* (New

Brunswick, NJ: Rutgers University Press, 1954), p. 479; McDonnell describes the Beguines as following a "via media"; pp. 120-140.

[12]Caroline Walker Bynum, "Religious Women in the Later Middle Ages," in *Christian Spirituality: High Middle Ages and Reformation*, ed. Jill Raitt (New York: Crossroad, 1987), p. 121.

[13]Ibid., pp. 59 ff.

[14]The classic biography is Paul Sabatier, *Life of St. Francis of Assisi* (London: Hodder and Stoughton, 1894). The earliest biographer was a contemporary, Thomas of Celano, who wrote two lives of Francis, available in *St. Francis of Assisi: Writings and Early Biographies* ed. Marion A. Habig (Chicago: Franciscan Herald Press, 1973), usually referred to as the *Omnibus of Sources*.

[15]See Cajetan Esser, *Origins of the Franciscan Order* (Chicago: Franciscan Herald Press, 1970), pp. 143-147.

[16]Little, *Religious Poverty and the Profit Economy*, p. 150.

[17]Cf. Leonardo Boff, *St. Francis*, pp. 55-56.

[18]Hinnebusch, *The History of the Dominican Order*, p. 28.

[19]Simon Tugwell, "Introduction," in his edited volume, *Early Dominicans* (New York: Paulist Press, 1982), p. 14.

[20]I Const., I, 4.

[21]See Brenda Bolton, *The Medieval Reformation* (London: Edward Arnold, 1983), p. 91.

[22]See Thomas J. Johnston, "Franciscan and Dominican Influences on the Medieval Order of Penance: Origins of the Dominican Laity," *Spirituality Today* 37 (1985) 108-119.

Notes Chapter 4

[1]WA VIII 573-669; See Francois Biot, *The Rise of Protestant Monasticism* (Baltimore: Helicon, 1963) for a thorough discussion of the various reformers views on monasticism, pp. 1-63.

[2]Calvin, *Institutes* IV, XIII, 20-21.

[3]Ibid, pp. 31-45.

[4]Ibid., p. 52.

[5]Augsburg Confession, no. XXVII, in *The Book of Concord*, translated and edited by Theodore G. Tappert (Philadelphia: Fortress Press, 1959), p. 80.

[6]See the La Rochelle Confession, Article XXIV; *Confessio helvetica posterior*, Chapter XVIII; Biot, pp. 58-59.

[7]See Raymond Hostie, *Vie et mort des Ordres reliqieux* (Paris, 1972), p. 166.

[8]Biot, *Protestant Monasticism*, pp. 65-67.

[9]According to George H. Williams, in his classic study, *The Radical Reformation* (Philadelphia: Westminster Press, 1962).

[10]See Timothy George, "The Spirituality of the Radical Reformation," in *Christian Spirituality: High Middle Ages and Reformation*, ed. Jill Raitt (New York: Crossroad, 1987), pp. 334-371.

[11] Ibid., p. 349; see also Biot's discussion of the Herrenhut Community in *Protestant Monasticism*, pp. 67-74.

[12] *The Autobiography of St. Ignatius of Loyola*, trans. Joseph F. O'Callaghan; ed. John C. Olin (New York: Harper & Row, 1974), p. 21; see also William V. Bangert, *A History of the Society of Jesus* (St. Louis: Institute of Jesuit Sources, 1966).

[13] For a translation and commentary see Jules Toner, "The Deliberation that Started the Jesuits," *Studies in the Spirituality of Jesuits* 6 (June 1974).

[14] See *The Constitution of the Society of Jesus*, trans. and ed. by George E. Ganss (St. Louis: Institute of Jesuit Sources, 1970).

[15] See Hostie, *Vie et Mort*, pp. 351-353.

[16] See Ruth P. Liebowitz, "Virgins in the Service of Christ: The Dispute over an Active Apostolate for Women During the Counter-Reformation," in *Women of Spirit*, ed. Rosemary Ruether and Eleanor McLaughlin (New York: Simon and Schuster, 1979), pp. 131-152.

[17] Claude Langlois, *Le catholicisme au féminin* (Paris: Cerf, 1984), p. 62.

Notes, Chapter 5

[1] See Rosabeth Moss Kanter, *Commitment and Community—Communes and Utopias in Sociological Perspective*, (Cambridge, MA: Harvard University Press, 1976).

[2] W. Loyd Allen, "Elements of Monastic Spirituality in Protestant Intentional Communities," *One in Christ* 19 (1983) 173.

[3] See Francois Biot, *The Rise of Protestant Monasticism* (Baltimore: Helicon, 1963); Olive Wyon, *Living Springs* (Philadelphia: Westminster Press, 1963).

[4] For liturgy in the Reformed tradition, see J.D. Benoit, *Liturgical Renewal* (London: SCM Press, 1958), pp. 30 ff.

[5] *The Book of Concord*, trans. and ed. Theodore G. Tappert (Philadelphia: Fortress Press, 1959), p. 710.

[6] See *Guide to the Religious Communities of the Anglican Communion* (London: A.R. Mowbray, 1955).

[7] *Le "tiers-ordre" protestant: Les Veilleurs* (Nantes, 10 July 1925).

[8] *L'Office Divin de chaque jour*, 2nd ed., (Delchaux & Niestlé, 1953).

[9] For the background on the Veilleurs and *Eglise et Liturgie* I am grateful to Robert Gribben's mimeographed text, "Liturgical Renewal in the Reformed Tradition: Can Anything Good Come Out of Geneva?" the Austin James Lecture, 1984, Ecumenical Liturgical Center, Melbourne, Australia.

[10] See Biot, *The Rise of Protestant Monasticism*, pp. 98-105.

Notes, Chapter 6

[1] See Kathryn Spink, *A Universal Heart: The Life and Vision of Brother Roger of Taizé* (New York: Harper & Row, 1986), also J.L. Gonzales Balado, *The Story of Taizé*, third revised edition (London & Oxford: Mowbray, 1988).

[2] Cited in Balado, *The Story of Taizé*, p. 23-24.

³Roger Schutz, *Parable of Community* (Oxford: Mowbray, 1980).

⁴See Jacques Berthier, *Music from Taizé* (Chicago: G.I.A., 1981).

⁵*Baptism, Eucharist and Ministry* (Geneva: WCC, 1982).

⁶See Roger Schutz, *The Power of the Provisional*, (Philadelphia: Pilgrim Press, 1969); also *Awakened from Within: Meditations on the Christian Life* (New York: Doubleday, 1987) which includes the rule of Taizé.

Notes, Chapter 7

¹See Michel Carrouges, *Soldiers of the Spirit: The Life of Charles de Foucauld* (New York: G.P. Putnam's Sons, 1956).

²See *Spiritual Autobiography of Charles de Foucauld*, ed. Jean-Francois Six (Denville, NJ: Dimension Books, 1964).

³René Bazin, *Charles de Foucauld* (Paris: Plon, 1921).

⁴See René Voillaume, *Seeds of the Desert: The Legacy of Charles de Foucauld* (Chicago: Fides, 1955).

⁵Soeur Magdeleine de Jésus, *Du Sahara au Monde Entier* (Paris: Nouvelle Cité, 1981).

⁶See Malcolm Muggeridge, *Something Beautiful for God: Mother Teresa of Calcutta* (Harper & Row: New York, 1971); Desmond Doig, *Mother Teresa: Her People and Her Work* (New York: Harper & Row, 1976; Kathryn Spink *The Miracle of Love: Mother Teresa of Calcutta, Her Missionaries of Charity, and her Co-Workers* (San Francisco: Harper & Row, 1981).

⁷*Perfectae caritatis*, no. 2, in *The Documents of Vatican II*, ed. Walter M. Abbott (New York: America Press, 1966), p. 468.

⁸See Donna Whitson Brett and Edward T. Brett, *Murdered in Central America*, (Maryknoll, NY: Orbis Books, 1988).

⁹For a contemporary approach to the religious life, see Sandra M. Schneiders, *New Wineskins: Re-imagining Religious Life Today* (New York: Paulist Press, 1986).

¹⁰Pope John Paul II addresses this tension in his letter to the U.S. Bishops, "Religious Life in the United States," *Origins* 18 (April 13, 1989) 747.

¹¹See Frédéric Lenoir, *Les communautés nouvelles* (Fayard, 1988).

Notes, Chapter 8

¹Mel Piehl's *Breaking Bread* (Philadelphia: Temple University Press, 1982) is an excellent study of the foundational role played by the Catholic Worker in the development of American Catholic social radicalism.

²See William D. Miller, *Dorothy Day: A Biography* (San Francisco: Harper & Row, 1982; also Jim Forest, *Love is the Measure* (New York: Paulist Press, 1986).

³Dorothy Day, *From Union Square to Rome* (New York: Arno Press, 1978).

⁴Cited in Piehl, *Breaking Bread*, p. 60.

⁵For a history of the Catholic Worker see William D. Miller, *A Harsh and Dreadful Love* (New York: Liveright, 1973).

⁶Sheila Durkin Dierks and Patricia Powers Ladley, *Catholic Worker Houses* (Kansas City, MO: Sheed and Ward, 1988).

⁷Piehl, *Breaking Bread*, p. 131.

⁸Cited by Ron Ferguson in *Chasing the Wild Goose: The Iona Community* (London: Collins/Fount Paperbacks, 1988), p. 58. I am endebted to Ferguson's book for the history of the community.

⁹Ferguson, *Chasing the Wild Goose*, pp. 198-99.

¹⁰See Michael Downey, *A Blessed Weakness: The Spirit of Jean Vanier and l'Arche* (San Francisco: Harper & Row, 1986).

¹¹Jean Vanier, "L'Arche: Its History and Vision," in *The Church and the Disabled Person*, ed. Griff Hogan (Springfield, IL: Templegate, 1983), p. 52.

¹²Vanier, "L'Arche: Its History," p. 59.

¹³Michael Downey analyzes Vanier's spirituality in "Jean Vanier" Recovering the Heart," *Spirituality Today* 38 (1986) pp. 337-48.

¹⁴See Jean Vanier, *Community and Growth* (New York: Paulist Press, 1989).

¹⁵See Wes Michaelson, "Crucible of Community," *Sojourners* 6 (January 1977) 14-21.

¹⁶For his personal story, see Jim Wallis, *Revive Us Again: A Sojourner's Story* (Nashville: Abingdon Press, 1983).

¹⁷Ibid., p. 4.

¹⁸Michaelson, "Crucible of Community," p. 16.

¹⁹For the story of one long time Sojourner Community member's involvement in the struggle for justice, see Joyce Hollyday, *Turning Toward Home* (San Francisco: Harper & Row, 1989).

²⁰Wallis, "Ten Years," p. 5.

²¹Wallis, "Ten Years," p. 4.

Notes Chapter, 9

¹See H. McKennie Goodpasture, *Cross and Sword: An Eyewitness History of Christianity in Latin America* (Maryknoll, NY: Orbis Books, 1989).

²See Enrique Dussel *A History of the Church in Latin America* (Grand Rapids, MI: William B. Eerdmans, 1981), pp. 50-55.

³For a good introduction to the struggle for justice and human rights in Latin America and for the conflict between the Catholic Church and U.S. policy, see Penny Lernoux, *Cry of the People* (New York: Penguin Books, 1982).

⁴See for example Leonardo Boff, *Ecclesiogenesis: The Base Communities Reinvent the Church* (Maryknoll, NY: Orbis, 1986) [first published in 1977]; also Julio de Santa Ana, "Schools of Sharing: Basic Ecclesial Communities" *The Ecumenical Review* 38 (1986) 381.

⁵Rosemary Ruether, "'Basic Christian Communities': Renewal at the Roots," *Christianity and Crisis* 41 (1981) 235.

[6]See Alvaro Barreiro, *Basic Ecclesial Communities: the Evangelization of the Poor* (Maryknoll, NY: Orbis Books, 1982).

[7]Julio de Santa Ana, "Schools of Sharing," p. 383.

[8]W.E. Hewitt, "Christian Base Communities (CEB's): Structure, Orientation, and Sociopolitical Trust," *Thought* 63 (1988) 173.

[9]Boff, *Ecclesiogenesis*, pp. 61-75.

[10]For some dated figures, see the appendix to Lernoux's *Cry of the People*.

[11]David Wilkerson, *The Cross and the Switchblade* (Westwood, NJ: Spire, 1964); for the story of the charismatic renewal in North America see Richard Quededeaux, *The New Charismatics II* (New York: Harper and Row, 1983).

[12]Kevin and Dorothy Ranaghan, *Catholic Pentecostals* (Paramus, NJ: Paulist Press, 1969).

[13]See Bertil W. Ghezzi, "Three Charismatic Communities," in *As the Spirit Leads Us*, ed. Kevin and Dorothy Ranaghan (Paramus, NJ: Paulist Press, 1971), pp. 164-186; also John O'Connor, "Covenant Communities: A New Sign of Hope," in *The Spirit and the Church*, ed. Ralph Martin (Paramus, NJ: Paulist Press, 1976), pp. 319-337.

[14]Mary Jo Neitz, *Charisma and Community: A Study of Religious Commitment within the Charismatic Renewal* (New Brunswick: Transaction Books, 1987), p. 27.

[15]Frédéric Lenoir, *Le communautés nouvelles* (Fayard, 1988).

[16]See Monique Hébrard, *Les nouveaux disciples: Voyage a travers les communautés charismatiques* (Centurion, 1979); also *Les nouveaux disciples dix ans aprés* (Centurion, 1987).

[17]See Killian McDonnell, "Eucharistic Exposition: An Obsolete Relic?" *America* 160 (February 25, 1989) 166-169.

[18]See for example Stephen B. Clark, *Building Christian Communities* (Notre Dame, IN: Ave Maria Press, 1972); also O'Connor, "Covenant Communities," pp. 332-333.

[19]Robert Cogswell, "The Church in Cuernavaca," *The Christian Century* 100 (1983) 1163.

[20]Josephine Massyngberde Ford, *Which Way for Catholic Pentecostals?* (New York: Harper and Row, 1976), pp. 40-64.

[21]Hewett, "Christian Base Communities," p. 174.

[22]Ibid., p. 167.

Notes, Chapter 10

[1]Mel Piel, *Breaking Bread: The Catholic Worker and the Origin of Catholic Radicalism in America* (Philadelphia: Temple University Press, 1982), p. 42.

[2]Jim Wallis, in Wes Michaelson, "Crucible of Community," *Sojourners* 6 (January 1977) 19.

[3]Sandra S. Schneiders, *New Wineskins: Re-imaging Religious Life Today* (New York: Paulist Press, 1986), pp. 32-33.

[4]See *The Crisis in Religious Vocations*, ed. Laurie Felknor (New York: Paulist Press, 1989).

⁵See M. Basil Pennington, "Temporary Monasticism," *America* 158 (April 9, 1988) 380-381.

⁶Monique Hébrard, *Les nouveaux disciples: Voyage a travers les communautés charismatiques* (Centurion, 1982), pp. 348-349.

⁷See "The Eucharist: Who May Preside?" *Commonweal* 115 (Sept. 9, 1988) 460-466.

⁸*Perfectae caritatis*, no. 1, in *The Documents of Vatican II*, ed. Walter M. Abbott (New York: America Press, 1966), p. 466.

⁹Pope John Paul II, "Religious Life in the United States," *Origins* 18 (April 13, 1989) 750.

Photo Credits

Page 61, Glen Jones, Abbey of New Clairvaux; page 169, *The Guardian,* Iona Community; page 199, Monastic Family of Bethlehem.

Pages 106-117: Nos. 1-9, Rausch; 10-13 Taizé; 14-15, Grandchamp; 16, Laura K. Martin, Missionary Brothers of Charity; 17, Missionary Brothers of Charity; 18-20, Los Angeles Catholic Worker; 21, L'Arche Tahoma Hope Community; 22, Rausch; 23-25, L'Arche Tahoma Hope Community; 26-27, Monastic Family of Bethlehem.

Subject Index